Table of Contents

UPGRADING YOUR PC
in easy steps

BRIAN AUSTIN

In easy steps is an imprint of Computer Step
Southfield Road . Southam
Warwickshire CV47 0FB . England

http://www.ineasysteps.com

Notice of Liability
Every effort has been made to ensure that this book contains accurate and current information. However, Computer Step and the author shall not be liable for any loss or damage suffered by readers as a result of any information contained herein.

Trademarks
All trademarks are acknowledged as belonging to their respective companies.

Printed and bound in the United Kingdom

ISBN 1-84078-094-0

Introduction to upgrading

Welcome to *Upgrading your PC in easy steps*. Upgrading a Personal Computer (PC) no longer needs to be left to the professionals. Many upgrading tasks can be completed by anyone armed with some basic knowledge about PCs – this book provides that knowledge.

This chapter explains what you need to get started and examines how the PC originated, including its development right up to the present day.

Covers

Chapter One

Introducing the PC

In August 1981, IBM changed our world forever with the launch of the first IBM PC, giving birth to a new industry standard.

Since then, millions of IBM PC-compatible Personal Computers (PCs) have been sold both in larger desktop size and smaller and lighter portable notebook format.

CPU speeds have evolved from a once-respectable 4.77MHz to the astounding 1.7GHz+ (1,700MHz) workhorses that are becoming ever more common today. You can learn more about the basic PC components on page 10.

So what's really in a PC? Today, most desktop PCs are made up of the following separate components, while portable notebook PCs have to contain all three in a single box:

The margins of this book include valuable information, hints, tips and additional guidelines to help you complete the job of upgrading more quickly and effectively.

Prepare in advance, stay focused, be patient and remain calm throughout your upgrading sessions. Oh, and try not to be interrupted!

- System unit: containing the CPU, motherboard, memory, hard drive, CD-ROM/DVD drive, floppy drive – and optionally Zip or SuperDisk drive, expansion cards, and so on.

- Display monitor: measured diagonally, 15" is now the most common size, but 17" and larger is preferable when working with Windows-based software.

- Keyboard and mouse: or other kinds of input and pointing devices.

From desktop to notebook in just a few short years!

On the buses

Information is moved between the major components in a PC using interconnecting links called buses. Different buses are used to meet different requirements. Expansion cards like sound cards fit into expansion slots which connect directly to the I/O or Input/Output bus for example.

Other buses in a PC include the data bus on which the information is moved, and the address bus which establishes where the data goes.

This book is not intended to replace instructions provided with your upgrades: the manufacturer's installation guides should always be followed and should be your first point of reference.

Most current PCs have 32 or 64-bit address buses, whereas older PCs might use a 16-bit address bus.

From an upgrade standpoint, we're mainly concerned with the I/O bus, otherwise known as the expansion bus. The original IBM PC provided the basis for the PC of today. Generally, PC makers needed to keep to the original PC specification to maintain backward-compatibility.

GigaByte GA-8TX

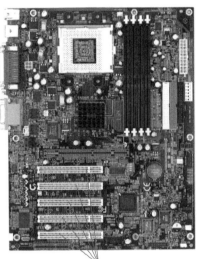

PCI bus expansion slots

Expansion slots come in several types, although today's PCs use the most common Intel-originated Peripheral Component Interconnect (PCI) bus. As the PCI bus is connected near to the CPU, it's often referred to as a local bus. The local bus concept provides one essential outstanding feature: speed.

To complete our overview of PC buses, earlier bus types included ISA/EISA (limited bus speed to a maximum of 8.33MHz data throughput), the MCA, PC Card and Vesa VL buses. For upgrading purposes though, you'll probably never come into contact with these older types.

Getting to know your PC

Here's a list of some important PC-related terms:

- Bit: an abbreviation of Binary digIT. A single binary number that is either 0 or 1 – the smallest building block necessary to create computer data.

- Byte: a collection of 8 bits. A byte is any single character, like the letter 'A' or number '9'.

- CPU: the main microprocessor chip or 'brains' of a PC. Modern CPUs contain millions of very fast electronic switches called 'transistors'.

- Gigabyte (Gb): is 1,073,741,824 bytes or characters (or about a thousand Megabytes).

- Hard drive: a very fast spinning disk on which information can be recorded (written) and accessed (read). A hard drive is a kind of long-term memory: information is kept intact after a PC is switched off.

- Kilobyte (Kb): is 1,024 bytes or characters (or 2^{10} bytes).

- Megabyte (Mb): is 1,048,576 bytes or characters (or about a thousand Kilobytes).

- PC bus: accepts expansion cards like a sound or video card, and allows your PC to include additional functions.

- Plug-and-Play (PnP): the PnP specification from Intel ensures that a range of different hardware devices, expansion cards and software can be set up to work together easily. Most new devices should be PnP-compatible. Look for the PnP logo.

- RAM: an acronym for Random Access Memory – used to store data temporarily and help with computer information processing. All information held in RAM is lost when a PC is switched off.

- Terabyte (Tb): for all practical purposes, is an extremely large amount of storage space or data! Compare with megabyte and gigabyte above.

Purchasing hardware upgrades

Common PC upgrading tasks include: installing extra memory (RAM), a larger hard drive, changing the motherboard, attaching a Zip disk, SuperDisk, CD-ROM or DVD drive, installing a faster video card, and so on. Furthermore, each major upgrade task may involve changing or updating further key parts in order to match the specification of latest key components.

For trouble-free upgrading, ensure each component you purchase matches the rest of your system properly. Some components may be listed as the same value in specification but may not be identical: check first.

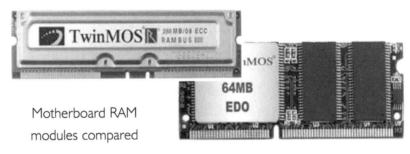

Motherboard RAM modules compared

Before starting your upgrade, make sure you have all the right screws, cables and connectors. Some upgrades may be supplied without connectors (like some hard drives for example). Check if you'll receive all that your need with your supplier at the time of purchase.

Avoiding incompatible products

To reduce the possibility of ending up with incompatible products after you've installed your upgrades, when you purchase your latest add-on for your PC, it's a good idea to identify to your supplier the other essential parts that make up your particular computer system.

For example, if you're purchasing a new second hard drive, make sure you know what type of motherboard is already fitted in your PC, the type and size of your existing hard drive, and so on. Check your PC's documentation.

If compatibility problems emerge later, by mentioning these facts to your supplier you've made compatibility an essential aspect of the contract of sale as defined by the Sale of Goods Act.

When interpreted strictly, this means if your upgrade can't work in your system, your supplier should not have sold it to you. However, be reasonable and look for the positive: the best suppliers automatically do their best to ensure your choice is compatible; it's simply good business! However, by checking with your supplier first before upgrading, you can avoid these kinds of problems.

Finding a competitive price

Many people use one or two favourite suppliers: if you've received good service in the past, then it makes sense to support these same suppliers. However, prices can vary considerably on some items. Therefore, often it's worth carrying out the following research:

- Check prices from a range of reputable sources to make sure your preferred supplier is competitive.

- Also, many suppliers now advertise 'price-matching', but will only do so if you can quote the alternative supplier and itemised details in their advertisement. So if you arm yourself with the appropriate knowledge before calling, you might save yourself some money.

Products from proven brand names often cost more. If product reliability is more important than price, it makes sense to purchase the best upgrades you can afford that match your existing system.

Don't forget the correct drivers

A software driver is an essential program that is often supplied with the hardware upgrade you're buying. Key point: it's essential that you have the correct driver for the product to work properly.

Windows 95/98/Me/XP and NT/2000 now come with many popular software drivers for a wide range of products.

However, software drivers are updated periodically, so make sure you know where you can obtain the latest updates. How: read the documentation that comes with your upgrade.

Iomega CD-RW drive

Many product makers provide access to their latest drivers on the Internet, through websites, newsgroups and various service providers. Online sources can provide an ideal solution to ensure you have the latest driver for your upgrade. Also, although unlikely, you may still be offered products that are not Year 2000 compliant: simply avoid these.

Some basic tools

Whether you're adding another component to your PC or simply upgrading an entire PC, you'll need access to some basic tools. The tools you'll need are usually inexpensive and are easily available from any hardware store, or you may be able to borrow what you need from a friend or neighbour.

Some computer-based retailers sell inexpensive compact kits containing the basic hand tools you'll need when upgrading your PC. Contact you local supplier.

However, some PC makers – Compaq included – use special star-shaped screws. For these, you may need a Torx-driver which fits sizes T10 and T15 Torx screws. Refer to your system manual and speak to your hardware shop's representatives about these special drivers if required.

Hand tools you'll probably need

For most of the tasks outlined in this book, you may need any of the following tools, depending on your particular system:

- Small Phillips-head screwdriver (#2)

- Small flat-head screw driver

- Medium Phillips-head screwdriver

- Medium flat-head screw driver

- Tweezers

- Small pliers

- Torch (essential when working in an average low-light domestic environment)

Any special tools you may need, like specific chip extractors (rarely needed now), are covered in the appropriate chapter, and are often available as part of an upgrade kit or from your computer supplier.

Other useful hand tools you may need

- CPU extractor tool (may come as part of a CPU kit)

- 3/16-inch nut spanner/driver (often used with IBM PCs)

- 1/4-inch nut spanner/driver (often used with IBM PCs)

Protecting yourself and your PC

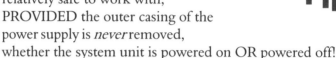

BEFORE REMOVING YOUR PC'S OUTER CASING, DISCONNECT THE MAINS POWER LEAD FROM THE PC.

Whenever anyone works on electrical equipment, there is always an element of risk or danger. The PC system box containing the motherboard is relatively safe to work with, PROVIDED the outer casing of the power supply is *never* removed, whether the system unit is powered on OR powered off!

While working with your PC, whether you're performing an upgrade or simply composing a letter, keep tea, coffee and any other drinks well away from your PC – and especially clear of the keyboard. Drinks can be spilt easily and may cause permanent damage, even if the PC is switched off at the time of spillage.

There should never be any need for anyone who is untrained to remove the outer casing of a PC power supply: these are designed to be replaced as a complete unit and should not need to be replaced often.

DANGER WARNING!

WITH THEIR CASINGS REMOVED, PC POWER SUPPLIES AND PC MONITORS CAN GIVE UNTRAINED USERS <u>A FATAL ELECTRICAL SHOCK, EVEN WHEN DISCONNECTED FROM THE MAINS SUPPLY</u>. DO NOT WORK ON THIS EQUIPMENT IF YOU ARE UNTRAINED – EVER!

Before refitting the outer casing to your PC, make sure you've refitted all screws into their correct locations and especially that no screws are trapped between the motherboard and PC casing.

Protecting your components from you

A static electrical charge can build up when any two surfaces are rubbed together. The human body can contain tens of thousands of volts. Luckily for us however, the electrical current is very small. Otherwise, we could be in for an interesting time couldn't we?

Static electricity represents a serious threat to your PC and any components you may be upgrading: you can damage the electronic devices you're installing simply by touching them. However, for a few pounds, you can buy an antistatic wrist strap kit. If used correctly, it can provide good protection for your PC and it's safe to use.

Before you start upgrading

Upgrading a PC can be straightforward if you understand what is required and follow the manufacturer's instructions. However, whenever you change a PC, there's always a risk that an accident may occur causing some damage or loss of data. Therefore, ALWAYS ensure that you have backed up all of your data before performing ANY upgrade.

If an entire backup is not possible, back up all essential files and data onto Zip disks/tape. If you don't feel confident that you can complete the upgrade, it's always better not to start; instead, contact a reputable service organisation to carry out the upgrade for you.

To learn more about PC fault-finding, why not check out: 'PC Troubleshooting in easy steps' available from Computer Step at: www.ineasysteps.com/

When upgrading your PC, take your time and perform each step carefully. Speed is not important: thoroughness is. Many potential problems can result simply from rushing. Fitting new modules is often not difficult first time, though does require some patience and a steady hand.

Some additional guidelines to consider

*   Never unplug the mains lead to your PC while it is switched on with your operating system working. Why? You could permanently damage your PC and files stored on its hard drive.

*   Before upgrading, tuck in any loose clothing like ties and remove your watch.

*   Take extra care and allow more time when working on or upgrading notebook PCs – especially if you need to remove the outer cover. Components are more closely packed and are more likely to become damaged easily.

*   Many computer upgrades are simpler than you may at first think. Although a PC is a 'high-tech' tool, performing basic tasks like adding more RAM memory or fitting a CD-ROM drive don't require complex skills, just a little care, some forethought and some basic guidance.

*   A range of technical support forums are available on the Internet and World Wide Web, packed with members who are usually very helpful. So if you experience an unusual problem, this may be a useful avenue to try. You may be pleasantly surprised at the outcome. Highly recommended is the PC Works mailing list – send an email with your question to: pcworks@mailinglist.net

Record all essential PC settings before starting

How: run MSD.exe (Microsoft Diagnostics), which is included on the Windows 98 CD-ROM in the \tools\oldmsdos\ directory or from the Microsoft website. Alternatively, use one of the specially designed diagnostic software packages available. Print and store the results in a safe place: this information may be useful for solving any problems that may occur later.

Disassembling and reassembling

Try to keep the various types of screws and connectors in some sort of order, so that you know which screws and connectors came from which part of your system. Always refit screws to their original locations. Keep user guides handy: you may need these when carrying out upgrades.

To quickly record all the settings in your BIOS SETUP, first set your printer ready to print. Then, with your BIOS SETUP information displayed, press the SHIFT+PRINT SCREEN buttons together. Do this for each section in your BIOS SETUP.

Know about your PC's BIOS setup

Your PC's SETUP program – the BIOS – stores key information about your PC. When you change a component in your PC, you may need to tell SETUP what you've done. Recent PCs usually update their BIOS automatically. Nevertheless it's always a good idea to know how to display your SETUP program and record the information it contains *before* starting to upgrade your PC.

How: read your PC user guide to discover how to display your BIOS data. Examples: in some PCs, you press the DELETE key or F1 key at the appropriate time during boot up after switching on; in others, you press the following key combinations: CTRL+ALT+ESC, or CTRL+ALT+S.

Installing and removing expansion cards

Take care when installing and removing expansion cards. Try not to apply too much pressure to the motherboard. Why: you may break the conductive tracks on the motherboard underside, result: ruined motherboard.

Make a drawing

Before changing your PC in any way, why not make a simple drawing of which expansion boards fit into which slots, which plugs go where, and so on?

All about motherboards

The motherboard is the heart of your PC and its key components play an important part in determining how fast your PC runs! In this chapter, we examine what a motherboard is and provide a strategy for choosing a motherboard. Finally, we outline the key tasks you need to perform when installing your new motherboard.

Covers

Chapter Two

Introduction to motherboards

What is a motherboard?

The motherboard – sometimes also referred to as the system board – is the skeleton of your PC, providing the framework that links all other central components together.

It's the main circuit board hosting your Central Processor Unit or CPU (example: Pentium); the 'chipset' – or control chips; RAM and ROM memory; several buses – or sets of interconnecting conductors – and the sockets or slots into which you plug expansion cards and other connectors.

Motherboard form factors

Until recently, motherboards were available in several popular forms: the older full-size AT, the Baby-AT, ATX, and the newer NLX form made up the main options available.

Today however, the ATX design seems to have become the predominant design, although there are variations like the Intel FlexATX and newer VIA iTX form.

Don't under-estimate the job of replacing a mother-board: it's a serious upgrade. The new board must be completely compatible with your existing system, the PC must be stripped down and the plug-in boards removed. Then all components refitted successfully.

The BIOS SETUP program is a part of the operating system that controls communications between your PC and its peripherals. The BIOS is usually stored in special Integrated Circuits (ICs) on the motherboard. However, some IBM PCs may use the hard drive to store the BIOS.

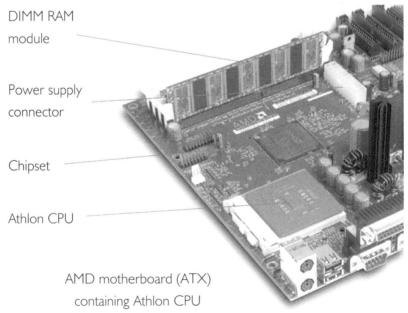

DIMM RAM module

Power supply connector

Chipset

Athlon CPU

AMD motherboard (ATX) containing Athlon CPU

In ATX designs, component layout was radically changed from the Baby-AT form to build in much needed improvements. On an ATX board, the CPU is sited further away from the expansion slots to make more room for full-length cards. From an upgrading standpoint, remember that an ATX board requires an ATX-compatible case *and* power supply.

For example, if you're upgrading from a Baby-AT form, in addition to the motherboard, you'll need to change the case, and probably CPU and RAM chips too.

The Accelerated Graphics Port

An AGP essentially helps speed up graphics performance in a PC and is particularly effective for displaying 3D moving components and playing full-motion videos more clearly.

Looking a little like a PCI expansion card slot, an AGP is accessible through its own connection socket on a motherboard.

Almost all new motherboards containing Accelerated Graphics Ports now run at 4x-speed (AGP 4). However, you'll need an AGP-compatible video card to take advantage of any AGP ports on your motherboard.

The AGP standard has developed into several levels starting originally with AGP-1x (slower), then AGP-2x (faster) and the current AGP-4x (fastest).

Power saving features

Most new motherboards include new features that enable key components to power down after a set period of inactivity. Advanced Power Management (APM) is one such feature that can simply set various components to a special Sleep mode: they can be 'woken up' easily using a mouse click or by pressing a key.

Obvious components affected include the display monitor and hard drive(s). An EnergyStar-compliant PC, for example, ensures that it uses less than 30 watts in Sleep mode (see page 97 for more information on this topic).

The Universal Serial Bus (USB) is now present on most new PCs with connecting sockets available on the outside casing. The USB system allows up to 127 devices to be connected and promises to make the job of attaching new peripherals to a PC much easier. The USB is also supported in Windows 98, Me, XP and NT/2000.

New motherboards will almost certainly use DIMM or RIMM to provide memory (RAM). If your motherboard uses the older SIMM-type memory modules, you'll almost certainly not be able (or not want to) use these in the new motherboard. To gain the most from a new motherboard, install appropriate fast memory also. Check with your supplier.

Buses and glue logic

A PC bus is an electronic pathway that carries common signals. Modern PCs use several types of bus to link the CPU, the motherboard memory (RAM) and any expansion cards like the video card and modem. For example:

- **Processor/CPU/ Front Side Bus (FSB):** the main communications channel between the CPU, the RAM and the chipset. Current speeds include: 66MHz, 100MHz, 133MHz, 200MHz and 266MHz. The latest Intel 850 chipset uses an incredible new 400MHz bus!

I/O or Input/ Output is a term that means data can be moved into and out of the CPU and the devices connected to it.

- **Peripheral Component Interconnect (PCI) bus:** runs at 33MHz – though a 66MHz version may still emerge. Most expansion cards now use PCI slots instead of the older ISA slots.

- **Accelerated Graphics Port (AGP) bus:** works with a video card to help speed up the display monitor. Requires an AGP-compliant video card inserted into the AGP slot. Most AGP buses now use AGP-4x mode which runs at an amazing 266MHz.

The new AMD Athlon CPUs feature Double Data Rate (DDR) speed-boosting technology to effectively double system bus speeds from 100MHz to 200MHz and 133MHz to an amazing 266MHz, or more!

- **Industry Standard Architecture (ISA) bus:** an older, slower 8.33MHz Input/Output (I/O) bus. Now little used.

- **Universal Serial Bus (USB):** allows for easy expansion or installation of add-ons without the need to physically install devices inside the PC. USB makes little demands on a PC, is fully supported in Windows 98, Me and XP, and up to 127 devices can be attached to the bus with data transfer speeds of up to 12Mbit/sec. The latest revision of USB – USB2 allows a whopping theoretical transfer rate of up to 480Mbps!

- **FireWire (IEEE-1394) bus:** another new fast I/O-type bus computer communications technology supported in Windows 98, Me, XP, NT and 2000, developed especially to handle the high demands of today's multimedia devices like DVD/CD-ROM drives, hard drives, and so on. Data can be moved at a speed of 400 Mb/sec, 800Mb/sec or even 3.2Gb/sec!

In addition to these main buses, most portable PCs like Notebooks include a PC Card bus to accept a wide range of add-on devices. More on PC Cards later.

The chipset or 'glue logic'

A motherboard's control ICs – or chipset – are also sometimes referred to as the 'glue logic', as these electronic 'chips' control the flow of data between the key parts of a motherboard. Key point: the type of chipset has a significant effect on your PC's overall performance. Motherboard design is usually centred around both a particular combination of chipset and CPU to ensure both are matched. Motherboards containing the most recent chipset are faster and therefore the preferable option to consider when buying. To ensure maximum performance, the motherboard RAM also has to match the chipset speed.

Installing a new, faster CPU won't necessarily provide you with a faster system. The important point here is that key components like motherboard, CPU, RAM, hard drive and video card need to be matched to each other to provide a balanced system. A balanced 1.33GHz system can actually run faster than a poorly balanced 1.5GHz PC.

Each device in a PC is connected to at least one bus and the chipset. Some devices actually link different buses together. Other buses include the address bus, data bus and memory bus.

The earlier Intel 440xx series was designed to run with the now older Pentium Pro and Pentium II/III CPUs, with the 440BX the first chipset to support both 66MHz and 100MHz motherboard bus speeds for the faster Pentium IIs/IIIs. Later chipsets included the Intel 450xx series for the Pentium Pro and Pentium II/Xeon CPUs.

Today's popular chipsets have to drive the new breed of very fast AMD Athlon and Pentium III and Pentium IV CPUs, and include the VIA Apollo Pro Plus, the latest Intel 8xx series – the most popular being the 810e, 815, 820 and 850 series – and the new AMD 760 series.

Mobile PCs typically use motherboards containing the SiS Motherboard Chipset, which supports Type II PC card slots and can drive screen sizes of up to 15 inches at 1400 x 1,050 resolution.

Choosing a motherboard

The fast pace of change in the PC industry today may mean that when changing a motherboard, you may also need to upgrade additional related components like the CPU, RAM and even the PC case/power supply at the same time.

Although there's a certain security in choosing a motherboard from a well known maker, some very good unbranded boards are available. Whatever make you decide to buy, do check their track record before purchase if you can. Get second opinions.

The quickest three ways to speed up a PC: 1. Install a faster CPU; 2. Add more RAM memory; 3. Upgrade the motherboard. However, each of these options may have implications which can affect the other two as all three need to be matched for best results.

Before buying, always let your supplier know the essential details of your PC, to ensure that your intended motherboard is fully compatible with the rest of your system and also to identify any potential problem areas.

Discover as much as you can about motherboards before deciding to purchase. Manufacturers' specifications and reviews in quality PC magazines offer a reliable indicator and are useful sources for related information. Note down a detailed specification requirement, so that you'll have all relevant information to hand when contacting suppliers. To start with, consider the following key guidelines:

Most current CPUs include some additional special memory bonded to the chip known as a cache. This Level 2 cache memory helps speed up a CPU, so the more Level 2 cache memory installed , the faster the relevant CPU runs. Current Intel Pentiums have 256Kb, the Celeron 128Kb, the AMD Athlon 256Kb and the Duron 128Kb.

- **CPU/Processor:** determine which CPU you want. Current options include: the Intel Pentiums III, IV and later versions, and the AMD Athlon and Duron CPUs.

- **CPU/Processor sockets/slots:** most new motherboards now use sockets: Socket 370 (PGA370) and Socket 423 for the latest Celeron/Pentium III/IV; plus Socket A for the latest AMD Athlon and Duron CPUs.

- **Motherboard form type:** currently, most new motherboards are available in ATX form only – which also requires an ATX case. So if you're upgrading from a Baby-AT motherboard to ATX, you'll almost certainly need to change the case/power supply too.

- **Motherboard speed:** get the fastest you can afford. Current choices include 66MHz, 100MHz, 133MHz (PC133), 200MHz and even 266MHz.

- **RAM type and speed:** are your existing RAM memory chips compatible? New motherboards usually accept DIMMs or the latest RIMMs but not the older SIMMs. Get the fastest RAM you can afford. Current speeds include 100MHz (PC100), 133MHz (PC133), 266MHz with Double Data Rate (DDR) and the incredible 800MHz (PC800) of the state-of-the-art RDRAMs from Rambus – expected to reach 1.2GHz by around 2005!

Most mother-boards now use 'flash-BIOS'. Result: the BIOS can be upgraded using a diskette/ CD-ROM, so you won't have to physically remove the PC's cover and change any electronic chips.

- **Chipset:** opt for the fastest and most up-to-date chipset that matches your CPU and RAM, and which at least supports: ATA-66 and ATA-100 hard drives, AGP-4x, and the current popular memory types: SDRAM DIMM and RDRAM RIMM.

- **BIOS:** is the BIOS supplier well-known and can the BIOS be upgraded with a disk (flash-BIOS)? Award, AMI, and Phoenix are three renowned BIOS providers. As a minimum, BIOS features should include: virus protection, power management, password options and, like the motherboard itself, should support the now well established Plug-and-Play (PnP) standard.

To gain the best speed advantage in a PC, ideally, buy as much RAM as you can afford. For Microsoft Windows 95, 98, Me, XP, NT and 2000, aim for a minimum of 128Mb – ideally 256Mb.

DIMMs and RIMMs are not interchangeable. They can be installed one at a time, not in pairs like the older SIMMs (see Chapter Four for more information).

- **Expansion cards/bus type:** can you use your existing expansion cards in your proposed new motherboard? You'll need at least 3 PCI slots (at version 2.1) and an AGP-4x slot (page 19). ISA cards are no longer used so you may also need to buy new PCI equivalents.

- **Interfaces/controllers:** choose a motherboard that comes with the maximum number and variety of interfaces and standard interface controllers built in. For example: 1.44Mb and 120Mb floppy disk support, E-IDE hard drive controllers, PCI local bus, 2 high speed serial ports, a USB port, ECP/EPP high speed printer port, PS/2 mouse port, SoundBlaster-compatible sound support, power management (APM), an Accelerated Graphics Port (AGP), networking, and ideally a built-in ASPI-compliant SCSI port.

Installing a motherboard

Before removing the old motherboard...

On Baby-AT motherboards, the power-supply connectors use two keyed plugs that are connected together. Note down which plug fits into which socket. When connected correctly, the black leads on each connector should usually be together in the middle of the pair.

These power connector leads should fit in only one way easily. However, it may be possible, with some force, to connect them the wrong way round, destroying your motherboard and probably other components too when you next switch on the PC. ATX motherboards use a special 20-pin keyed power connector which is virtually impossible to insert wrongly.

Here's an easy way to unclasp a plastic support holding a motherboard: push an empty Biro (insides removed) down over the clasping tags to compress all the plastic tags at once. Then, gently pull the plastic support from the other side. Repeat for each support.

Motherboards are particularly sensitive to electrostatic discharge. Take the precautions outlined in Chapter One to minimise the danger from static. You can damage an electronic card or motherboard through static electricity even though it may continue functioning perfectly for a while.

To remove the old motherboard

1 Note the configuration of all connectors and plug-in boards.

2 Carefully remove all plug-in expansion/adaptor cards and unplug all connectors.

3 Unscrew and remove any screws holding the motherboard, noting which holes are used.

4 Slide out the motherboard with the plastic standoffs still attached and place the motherboard on a table away from your work area.

Setting up your new motherboard

Often, a motherboard may work over a range of frequencies to allow for different CPUs, etc. Current motherboards – for Socket 370, Socket A, Slot 1, Slot 2, and Slot A – should automatically configure themselves.

However, older motherboards may need setting manually, usually by installing or removing small links called 'jumpers'. You can set the CPU type, speed and voltage; expansion bus speed; clock multiplier; and amount of cache memory fitted. However, always refer to your motherboard's user guide for precise details. Make sure all jumpers are positioned correctly before switching on.

Again, for older motherboards only, you may also need to manually update the information in your PC's SETUP program or BIOS, to tell it about the changes you've made and the frequencies chosen. Check your motherboard's user guide for details. The latest motherboards now configure themselves automatically, making the job much easier.

To install the new motherboard

1 Set all jumpers or switches correctly if necessary.

2 (Optional) Install any SIMM, DIMM, RIMM, CELP, or COAST modules.

3 Insert plastic standoffs in the correct positions and reinsert the motherboard. Make sure all plastic standoffs are sited correctly and that no screws are jammed between the motherboard and PC case.

4 Secure the holding screws holding the motherboard. Carefully reinstall all connectors and expansion cards (see notes below).

Although Windows 95, 98, Me, XP, 2000 and NT support Advanced Power Management (APM), for APM to actually work, all the relevant hardware and software must also be APM-compatible.

Refitting your expansion cards

Carefully fit the essential cards first, like your video card if required. Take care when refitting all plug-in expansion cards: try not to apply too much pressure and bend the motherboard excessively. If you need to apply firmer pressure when inserting cards, support the bottom of the motherboard with some thick layers of cardboard or other suitable material (not your hand).

Make sure that nothing is obstructing a card: it's easy to lose stray screws, so make sure none are lying in an expansion slot before you try to reinsert your expansion card. After checking your work thoroughly, switch on, test, make sure the PC starts up correctly and your hard drive works normally. Then switch off and refit any other remaining cards.

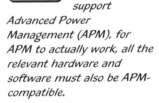

The Setup BIOS

Motherboards contain a special set of memory chips quite separate from the 'main' memory made up of SIMMs, DIMMs, and now RIMMs that are used for loading and running applications.

This extra memory is for the BIOS – Basic Input Output System. BIOS information may be stored partly in ROM and partly in CMOS RAM (NVRAM). To complicate matters further, additional BIOS commands are often stored in electronic chips on expansion cards – video, SCSI or network cards for example.

The BIOS is very important; without it, nothing in your PC would work. It stores information about things like your hard drive(s); the types of floppy disk drives installed; the amount and type of memory, and so on. When the PC is first switched on, the BIOS comes into play, checks the memory and performs other system checks. If the BIOS checks are successful, the operating system then loads.

ROM – Read Only Memory – keeps its information intact even when the PC is powered off. For information to remain stored in CMOS RAM however, it must be maintained by a backup battery or special capacitor when the PC is turned off.

The BIOS in ROM

The ROM BIOS chips usually contain the POST or Power On Self Test sequence and an option which can allow you to enter the BIOS SETUP program by pressing a key or key combinations. In modern Plug-and-Play-compliant motherboards, the ROM BIOS may also contain other instructions to assign Plug-and-Play computer resources.

The ROM BIOS examines the hard drive first, then, if necessary, the CD-ROM or floppy drive. Once the ROM BIOS tests are successful, the PC tries to load the operating system. If no operating system is accessible, the ROM BIOS usually displays a message on the screen prompting you to insert an operating system boot disk into one of the drives.

The Setup BIOS in CMOS RAM

The CMOS RAM stores information specific to your PC, like the size and quantity of hard and floppy drives, how much memory is installed, the time and date, and so on. Today, most BIOS chips will auto-detect hard drives. When you upgrade, you may need to enter the BIOS SETUP program to tell the PC what you've done.

Central Processing Units (CPUs)

One of the simplest and most effective ways to speed up your PC is to upgrade to a faster CPU. However, a CPU must be compatible with your motherboard. In this chapter, we examine the types of CPU available, CPU alternatives, and the issues to consider if you're thinking of upgrading. Finally, we outline how to fit a replacement CPU.

Covers

Chapter Three

Introducing the CPU

The Central Processing Unit (CPU), or Processor, is the brains of your PC, performing all the essential number-crunching and information processing. It does this through the use of **input** devices (keyboard, mouse), **output** devices (display monitor, printer) and **storage** devices (RAM, hard drives).

The CPU is the single most important component that has the most influence on a PC's overall performance.

A CPU keeps the processing of data in step using an extremely fast clock. Early CPUs worked in the kilohertz (KHz) range, whereas current Pentium IVs and AMD Athlons clock data at speeds of around 1.7GHz or more – that's 1,700MHz or 1,700 million times each second!

AMD Duron CPU

Before buying your new CPU/ motherboard, to help build in some future-proofing, check what the current trend is – sockets or slots – and keep to it. Why: if you make the wrong choice and want to upgrade again in say 12 months, you might have to replace both the CPU and motherboard, instead of just one of them.

A CPU's complexity is reflected in its cost; it is easily the most expensive IC (Integrated Circuit) on the motherboard. Upgrading, therefore, should be considered carefully. Although alternatives do exist, the dominant CPUs are now the Intel Pentium III/IVs, Intel Celerons, AMD Athlon and AMD Duron.

64-bits – and rising: today's standard

Current CPUs like the Pentium III/IV and AMD Athlon/Duron are optimised for 64-bit operation externally and 32-bit operation internally – to match most current software and operating systems like Windows 95, 98, Me, XP, NT and 2000.

Intel Pentium 4 CPU with Intel 850 chipset

Sockets, slots and CPU packaging

Most CPUs were originally designed for installing in sockets fixed to the motherboard. Later, CPU designs moved to slots as the preferred installation method. However, at the time of writing, the trend is moving back to sockets again.

CPU packaging refers to the way in which a CPU looks and how it connects to the motherboard. Current generation CPUs are available in at least two types:

- **Pin Grid Array (PGA) or Staggered Pin Grid Array (SPGA):** uses **sockets**. Examples include Socket 370 (PGA-370 – 370 pins) for the current standard Pentium III/ IV and Celeron CPUs, and Socket A (462 pins) for the current generation of AMD Athlon and Duron CPUs.

- **Single Edge Connector (SEC):** uses **slots** – designed for the earlier Pentium II/IIIs and variants plus AMD Athlons. A SEC is a small electronic circuit board that plugs vertically into the motherboard using one of several special connectors: Slot 1 (SC242 – 242 pins) and Slot 2 (SC330 – 330 pins) served the earlier Pentium II, Pentium III, Xeon and Celeron CPUs, and Slot A (242 pins) for earlier AMD Athlon CPUs.

One of the latest super fast CPUs from Intel: the Itanium

Types of CPU

Current CPU favourites

Below is a list of current popular CPUs. Most are available in a range of speeds, for both standard desktop and mobile PCs:

- **Intel Pentium III:** may soon become dated.

- **Intel Pentium IV:** currently, Intel's 'flagship' product, available in a range of speeds currently up to about 1.8GHz. The latest Intel Itanium has just been released.

- **AMD Athlon:** currently available in speeds of up to 1.8GHz.

- **Intel Celeron:** a Celeron is simply a Pentium with less built-in memory – only 128Kb of Level 2 cache instead of the standard 256Kb. However, Celeron CPUs cost considerably less to manufacture, and therefore to buy, than their almost equivalent Pentiums, so offer superb value for money. Specially adapted Mobile Celerons are also available for the more tightly packed portable PCs.

- **AMD Duron:** equivalent to the Intel Celeron and available in a range of speeds.

CPU cache is a special type of memory bonded onto a CPU. The more cache memory a CPU has, the faster it runs. Current CPUs typically use 128Kb and 256Kb of Level 2 cache, but CPUs with 512Kb of faster Level 3 cache are soon to follow.

The older Intel Pentium II Xeon CPU

An older Intel Pentium II slot-mounted CPU with heat sink

Intel Pentium Overdrive processor: previously popular on early Pentium motherboards

An AMD Athlon ATX motherboard and CPU

The manufacturing process that results in today's PCs is simply quite amazing. Component parts that make up current CPUs and motherboard chipsets are extremely small – typically 0.18 microns wide and getting smaller. Compare that to the width of a human hair which is about 100 microns!

New, super fast processors: the Intel Itanium

Although the Intel Pentium 4 processor is now established, Intel, at the time of writing, ever looking over the next 'hill' have announced their latest CPUs: the 64-bit Itanium and Mckinley – to emerge soon. These 'high-end' CPUs are initially targeted at high-performance processing applications on a range of popular operating systems.

The Explicitly Parallel Instruction Computing (EPIC) design enables the Itanium to handle terabytes of information extremely fast. Initially, CPU speeds of 733MHz and 800MHz are expected to be available, with faster processors coming later.

The future just around the corner

At the time of writing, Intel has claimed to have made a breakthrough in design that will allow CPUs to reach speeds of up to about 20GHz. So how is it to be done? Answer: by packing more into the same space.

Intel say these new CPUs will use tiny transistors of 0.02 microns – compare that with a typical equivalent transistor today of 0.18 microns! However, we might have to wait a few years before these super fast CPUs become available in 'off-the-shelf' PCs.

Choosing a CPU

When deciding which CPU to buy, currently the safest route is to choose between the Intel Pentium or Celeron, or the AMD Athlon or Duron series. Other choices will also become available as new CPUs are developed. Both Intel and AMD are well established and have proven products.

Intel Pentium

For the Intel Pentium series, we suggest you consider the following options:

If you are unsure, always check exact CPU compatibility with your supplier. Why: to avoid any possible damage to a CPU and the motherboard by making the wrong choice.

- **Intel Pentium III:** ideally, seek a CPU of at least 933MHz

- **Pentium IV:** opt for at least 1.4GHz

- **Pentium Celeron:** to make the upgrade worthwhile, ideally choose a speed of at least 700MHz

AMD CPUs

The AMD Athlon is designed to compete directly with the Pentium IIIs and IVs, and the AMD Duron is offered as an alternative to the Pentium Celeron.

Upgrading the CPU on most (especially older) notebook PCs is not usually possible as the CPU may be bonded to the motherboard deep inside the casing. However, upgrading the RAM or hard drive can often be done easily, without the need to remove the outer cover. Check your documentation and discuss options with your dealer.

- **AMD Athlon:** current speed recommendation: get an Athlon with a speed of at least 1GHz

- **AMD Duron:** ideally, opt for at least 800MHz

Alternative CPU upgrade options

Some earlier Pentium and Pentium II motherboards can also be upgraded using various upgrade kits. However, although these kinds of upgrades may be cheaper, you need to be sure that your particular system can be upgraded properly, and that the upgrade is worthwhile. A range of upgrade kits is available from Evergreen, for example. Discuss options with your dealer.

Installing a CPU

Slotted CPUs are now almost obsolete and most new motherboards hold the CPU using a socket – either Socket A for AMD CPUs or Socket 370 for Intel CPUs. However, given the fast-paced development of the PC, these kinds of trends can change or reverse quickly.

Installing a CPU in a Zero Insertion Force (ZIF) socket

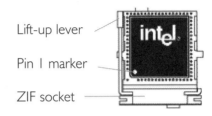

Lift-up lever

Pin 1 marker

ZIF socket

Take care when inserting a CPU. Insert the CPU pins into the correct holes in the CPU socket – the CPU should 'drop' in easily. If a CPU is inserted incorrectly or misaligned, when you power up, the PC will not work and the CPU and/or motherboard will probably both be destroyed. Other components may also be damaged.

Some new motherboards can be bought with a new CPU already installed, reducing the risk of damage to the CPU or motherboard during your upgrade.

Most motherboards use a Zero Insertion Force (ZIF) socket to hold the CPU. Therefore, changing the CPU is a simple job. After switching off the PC, disconnecting from the mains supply and taking electrostatic precautions, do the following:

1 If the CPU has a heat sink clamped to its top, carefully undo the heat sink clamps.

2 Raise the ZIF retaining lever.

3 Carefully lift/remove the original CPU. Place the CPU away from the work area with pins facing upwards.

4 Prepare the new CPU by carefully removing it from its packaging and align pin 1 on the CPU with pin 1 on the socket. Usually, this means aligning the dot or notched corner with the socket corner situated at the base of the handle, or the corner where the pin holes are different to those of the other corners.

5 Carefully push the new CPU securely into its ZIF socket and lower the retaining handle to lock the CPU into place.

6 Set any jumpers to the correct positions.

7 Reinstall the heat sink if required. Remember, adequate cooling is *essential* for fast CPUs.

Installing a CPU into a SEC slot

Earlier Pentium II/IIIs came in Single Edge Connector (SEC) packaging and use special vertical mounting brackets/plastic heat sink supports, that also help align and secure the CPU properly into the slot on the motherboard. You can then secure the SEC properly using special retaining clips. The CPU mounting brackets are usually supplied as part of the motherboard purchase.

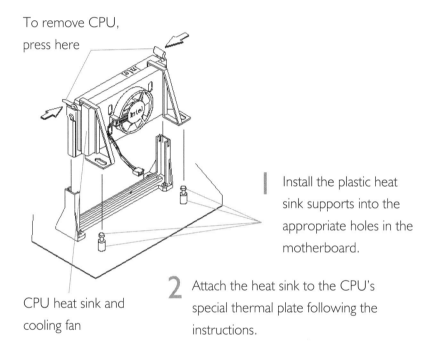

To remove CPU, press here

CPU heat sink and cooling fan

1 Install the plastic heat sink supports into the appropriate holes in the motherboard.

2 Attach the heat sink to the CPU's special thermal plate following the instructions.

Memory devices

Random Access Memory (RAM) plays an essential part in your PC: nothing would work without it. Adding more RAM is also one of the cheapest ways of speeding up a PC. In this chapter, we examine exactly what RAM is, the different types of RAM currently available, and tackle some of the problems you might be faced with if you want to install more RAM in your PC.

Covers

Chapter Four

Introducing RAM

RAM, or Random Access Memory, is used as a temporary storage area for holding information or making calculations while you're using your PC.

RAM is often referred to as volatile – this means that it will only remember information while the PC is switched on. Once the power is removed, information held in RAM is lost. By using a program's 'Save' command, you can copy any data you want to keep to the hard drive for easy access later.

The amount of RAM in a PC can significantly affect how fast your PC works and is measured in megabytes (Mb). Microsoft Windows 95, 98, Me and XP like at least 32Mb of motherboard RAM, preferably 64Mb or more, for 'comfortable' operation.

Windows 2000 works best with at least 128Mb of RAM – 256Mb is a better option if your budget will allow. Consequently, many new PCs are now being supplied with 64Mb or 128Mb as standard.

The speed of RAM traditionally used to be measured in nanoseconds. So in older specification sheets for example, you might see a memory module as 32Mb, 60ns.

Nowadays however, RAM speed is usually measured in megahertz (MHz) – typically 100MHz (PC100), 133MHz (PC133) right up to 800MHz (PC800) for the latest RIMM memory.

A byte is a term used in computers to indicate the storage space needed to create a single character like an 'A' or '1'. A byte is usually made up of 8 'bits' – a 'bit' being the smallest storage measurement in computing (0 or 1).

Kb (kilobyte) is a measure of data capacity for hard drives, and is 2^{10} bytes (1,024 bytes) not 1,000 bytes.

Mb (megabyte) is also a measure of data capacity, and is 2^{20} bytes (actually 1,048,576 bytes), not 1,000,000 bytes.

Types of RAM

Two common RAM forms are used in PCs today: static RAM (SRAM) and dynamic RAM (DRAM). Once an SRAM cell has received information, it can keep the information intact without any further action being required, provided electrical power is maintained. SRAM is very fast but expensive to produce so tends to be used for cache memory within the Pentium III/IV, Celeron, AMD Athlon and Duron CPUs.

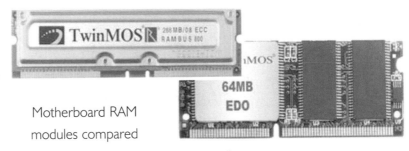

Parity is a method used in memory ICs to check whether information received is correct. Several years ago, parity was commonly used in the better quality memory chips and both SIMMs and DIMMs are available with or without parity. Currently however, most PCs do not use parity-checking. When upgrading, to be sure, always check with your supplier or motherboard manufacturer to make sure you buy the correct type of memory module.

Motherboard RAM modules compared

DRAM is entirely different to SRAM. A DRAM memory cell requires constant 'refreshing' to maintain the data and this happens at a very fast rate. DRAM uses fewer transistors when compared to SRAM and so DRAM memory is usually cheaper to produce. DRAM is usually used to create the motherboard memory modules outlined below.

DIMMs and RIMMs

Today, most RAM is available as plug-in modules that attach to a motherboard, in the form of Dual Inline Memory Module (DIMM) and the Rambus Inline Memory Module (RIMM) format. Neither is interchangeable so each must be installed in its own socket. Careful design has ensured that DIMMs and RIMMs can only be inserted easily one way around so that pin 1 on the module correctly connects to pin 1 on the appropriate socket.

RIMM is the fastest, most recent innovation in plug-in memory for PCs that use Rambus DRAM (RDRAM). With 184 pins, RIMMs are currently available in a range of capacities including 32Mb, 64Mb, 128Mb, 256Mb and larger.

Special, more compact varieties of DIMM and RIMM have also been developed for use with portable PCs and notebook computers. Look for names like Small Outline Dual Inline Memory Module (SO-DIMM) and Small Outline Rambus Inline Memory Module (SO-RIMM).

DIMMs, with 168 pins, usually contain Synchronous DRAM (SDRAM) chips, and are also currently available in a range of capacities including 32Mb, 64Mb, 128Mb, 256Mb and 512Mb.

Most current SDRAMs run at a speed of 100MHz or 133MHz. However, a more recent design uses a technique called Double Data Rate to double the speed to 200MHz and 266MHz respectively.

Like the latest RIMMs, these latest DDR SDRAMs also have 184 pins. However, even the boosted speed of DDR SDRAMs does not match the most recent RIMM speeds of 800MHz+, suggesting that RIMM designs look set to be the RAM of choice at least for the near future.

If you use Microsoft Office on Windows 2000 or later, I recommend you fit 128Mb or more of RAM to ensure a reasonable response. Ideally, opt for at least 256Mb – more if you use demanding CAD or video editing softare.

SIMM: an older type of RAM memory

Before DIMMs became available, the Single Inline Memory Module (SIMM) was the preferred format for several years. Later, faster SIMMs had 72 pins, while earlier slower versions used 30 pins, and both had to be installed in pairs. SIMMs are essentially obsolete now as almost all new motherboards will only accept DIMM or RIMM modules, each of which can be installed singly.

Example of an earlier, high-capacity SIMM: memory capacity = 32Mb; number of pins = 72; response time = 70ns

Choosing RAM

Gold or tin?

Computer signals run at very high frequencies and the higher the frequency, the more important it is to have a secure electrical connection.

The Supermicro P5MMA ATX motherboard

A typical motherboard could contain two SIMM banks, designated Bank 0 and Bank 1; on this motherboard, two SIMM sockets make up one SIMM bank

Credit card-type memory comes in various types. Fit the wrong type into your notebook and you could damage it beyond repair. To ensure your proposed credit card-type memory is compatible with your PC and the systems you want to work with, consult with your notebook supplier or manufacturer.

Two 168-pin DIMM sockets; each DIMM socket makes up one bank

Both SIMMs and DIMMs are available with gold- or tin-plated contacts. If you mix them, the electrical connection at high frequencies may become affected over time.

Therefore, when choosing or upgrading your RAM, make sure the SIMM or DIMM you choose matches the socket type on your motherboard. So either gold to gold or tin to tin, and not gold to tin or tin to gold.

For RIMMs, the problem is avoided as both RIMM contacts and their sockets are gold-plated.

Direct Rambus RIMM

Installing motherboard RAM

To add more RAM memory to a PC, you have three options:

- Add more RIMMs, DIMMs or SIMMs to any vacant memory slots on your motherboard.

- Replace existing memory with larger capacity memory modules.

- You may be able to add a memory expansion card – however, this is the least preferable solution, as the memory may then be limited by the bus speed of your motherboard – which may mean a significant loss in performance if the motherboard is older than about three years.

Upgrading the CPU on most notebook PCs is not usually possible as the CPU may be bonded to the motherboard deep inside the casing. However, upgrading the RAM or hard drive can often be done easily, without the need to remove the outer cover. Check your documentation and discuss options with your dealer.

Memory banks

When fitting motherboard RAM, you also need to know the bank layout on your motherboard. Memory must be fitted in banks starting with bank 0, then bank 1, bank 2, and so on.

Each bank must be full before the PC can use the bank. Most new Pentium-based PCs now use 168-pin DIMMs each of which uses a single bank of memory, making the job of upgrading easier than with the older SIMMs. Usually, two SIMMs were required to fill a single bank.

SIMMs must be installed in pairs, whereas DIMMs and RIMMs can be installed singly. Also, make sure the memory you buy is fully compatible with your system.

RAM speed

Motherboard RAM has to at least match the speed of the motherboard clock. Current typical RAM speeds for DIMMs include 100MHz, 133MHz and, for Double Data Rate DIMMs, 200MHz and 266MHz. Also, the latest RIMMs run at 800MHz or more. Upgrading older SIMMs may simply no longer be economical.

Choosing DIMMs

Choose a DIMM which is designed specifically for the target PC: a 'general' DIMM may not have the correct specifications. Also, remember that most motherboards do not accept both SIMMs and DIMMs used together.

Evaluating how much RAM memory you can add

Make sure that the memory you install is compatible with your motherboard's chipset and CPU and that any new RAM matches the motherboard's bus speed – currently: 66MHz, 100MHz, 133MHz, 200MHz, 266MHz, or 800MHz.

When upgrading the RAM on your PC's motherboard, whether you're adding more RAM or replacing one type of RAM with another, you need to identify the RAM already installed. You need to know what type it is, how fast it runs, whether it is parity or non-parity, and so on. Establishing the type of motherboard enables you to discover the options available to you when upgrading.

If your PC uses special proprietary RAM then you may have to install the type specified. Check with your supplier or PC manufacturer. To determine how much memory you can add, consider the following guidelines:

Upgrading the RAM in many recent notebook PCs is now much easier. Often, you need only remove a single screw on the casing to reveal a special slot area that can accept SO-DIMM or SO-RIMM memory. However, the correct type of memory is required. Discuss options with your supplier. Upgrading older portable PCs that require complete cover removal may not be economical.

- What is the total amount of RAM you want to install: 64Mb, 128Mb, 256Mb, 384Mb, or greater?

- How many RIMM, DIMM or SIMM slots does your motherboard have? Most motherboards do not have more than four of each type.

- How much RAM is already installed: typically 32Mb, 64Mb, 128Mb, or 256Mb? In Microsoft Windows, you can double-click the 'System' icon in the Control Panel to determine the current RAM installed.

- Are any slots empty? If your motherboard has three slots and two slots each have a 64Mb DIMM installed, you may be able to install another 128Mb DIMM in the remaining slot to make a total of 256Mb (see Hot Tip in margin). If no slots are empty, and you want more memory, and if your PC can accept a greater amount of total RAM, you'll have to buy larger capacity DIMM or RIMM modules, then remove and discard the existing smaller capacity RAM modules.

Installing and removing SIMMs, DIMMs and RIMMs

Before starting, make sure the power is off and you've connected your antistatic wrist strap. Inserting or removing a SIMM, DIMM or RIMM module is a simple job but do take care. Both use a similar locking mechanism to hold the memory modules in place and so installing and removing involve similar routines. The steps below are for guidance purposes only: follow the exact instructions supplied with your SIMM, DIMM, RIMM or motherboard.

To install a SIMM, DIMM or RIMM

Take special care when inserting and removing RAM. If the clips each side of the SIMM, DIMM or RIMM that hold the module in place break, your PC may display memory errors. Why: for reliable operation, the very high frequency electronic signals used in PCs demand a 100% 'solid' connection.

1 Orientate the SIMM/DIMM/RIMM so that it is facing the correct way before inserting. The module will fit in easily only one way, so don't force it.

2 Pull open the plastic anchors at each side of the SIMM/DIMM/RIMM socket.

3 Gently insert the SIMM/DIMM/RIMM into its socket. You may need to insert a SIMM at an angle of about 45 degrees to the vertical. Insert a DIMM/RIMM vertically (usually).

Any empty RIMM sockets must have a continuity module inserted. If unsure, check your PC documentation or discuss this topic with your supplier.

4 Push the tabs at each side of the SIMM socket outwards, while pushing the SIMM into position vertically until the tabs at each end of the socket lock the SIMM into place. When you insert a DIMM/RIMM, the action usually pulls the two anchors on each end of the DIMM/RIMM back into place.

To remove a SIMM, DIMM or RIMM

1 Carefully push or pull the tabs on each side of the SIMM/DIMM/RIMM socket outwards.

2 Pull the SIMM/DIMM/RIMM up carefully and remove from the socket. You may need to gently rock the SIMM/DIMM at an angle to remove it easily.

Hard drives

The hard drive is the workhorse of your PC, performing the amazing feat of storing huge amounts of information. However, it's astounding how quickly space on a hard drive can become used up. Sometimes, the simplest answer is to install a second hard drive. This chapter examines hard drive specifications, and explains how to install a new hard drive and complete the necessary related tasks.

Covers

Chapter Five

Hard drive overview

The hard drive maintains your data when the PC's power is switched off. Most computers have at least one hard drive called drive C: – additional hard drives are usually called drive D:, E:, F:, and so on. Modern hard drives are sealed (though not airtight) units usually containing several rigid circular platters or disks, close to which several moveable recording heads read and write (store)

The positioning of jumpers on a hard drive determines whether the drive is a master or slave device and therefore its status. Always check the drive's status, even if the maker says the drive is already set.

Don't move or knock a PC while it is switched on: PC hard drives are vulnerable to vibration and fragile, especially while powered up. Why? The hard drive read/write heads run extremely close to the drive platters. With newer hard drives, when a PC is switched off however, automatic head-parking moves the read/write heads safely away from the main data area.

A typical modern hard drive shown with the outer casing removed

Multiple recording platters

Read-write head assembly

data, with controller circuitry that now usually comes built in to the drive casing. Hard drives now come in two main forms:

- **SCSI (pronounced 'scuzzi'):** SCSI drives can also be further divided into further types including: SCSI II, Wide, Fast, and a few other types also.

- **IDE:** currently also available in two varieties: E-IDE and the new faster Ultra DMA.

How data is stored on a hard drive

Information is stored in tracks, cylinders and sectors. Data is stored on both sides of each platter, in concentric circles known as **tracks**. Each track can be divided up into set amounts called **sectors**. All tracks of the same type from every platter vertically are referred to as a **cylinder**.

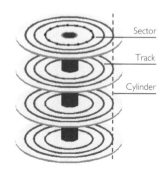

Sector

Track

Cylinder

IDE and Enhanced IDE (E-IDE)

Western Digital hard drive

Master/Slave jumper pins

Data connector socket (IDE)

Power connector socket

Early IDE drives could only reach a maximum size of 528Mb and accommodate only two IDE hard disks. IDE drives have now been made obsolete by E-IDE drives. With the most recent ATA-4/5 specification, E-IDE allows for hard drives up to 137Gb+. Above 8.4Gb, E-IDE uses a fast system of data access called Logical Block Addressing (LBA). Several speeds or 'modes' are possible, divided into modes 3, 4 and 5. Mode 5 drives are not yet in common use, so mode 4 is the fastest currently available, providing up to 16.6M/sec of data throughput.

Also with E-IDE, the concept of channels was introduced, providing two hard drive channels, each of which allows up to two devices – like CD-ROM/DVD-ROM drives, hard drives and tape drives – to be connected to the motherboard.

IDE Ultra DMA hard drives

Ultra DMA drives are the latest, fastest hard drives currently available using the Ultra DMA/66 and Ultra DMA/100 speeds (see overleaf).

SCSI hard drives

SCSI, pronounced 'scuzzi', is another very fast standard by which PCs access data. Originally, SCSI supported up to eight devices (called SCSI IDs). The older SCSI-2 standard is designed for easy connection and attachment of up to 15 devices, including printers, plotters, and scanners. The current SCSI-3 series is still in development.

Hard drive capacity is measured in millions of bytes. One megabyte of RAM, however, refers to 2^{20} which equates to 1,048,576 bytes, where each 'byte' is equal to 8 'bits' of data.

The 'sustained transfer' rate is one of the most important specifications used to describe the performance of a hard drive. It's a measure of the amount of data a drive can continuously read or write, and is measured in megabytes per second (Mb/sec).

Choosing a hard drive

Today, hard drives represent superb value for money. In recent years, prices have dropped dramatically while drive capacities have increased and data access times shortened. Nevertheless, modern operating systems, applications software and data files seem to take up more space than ever before. Remedy: when upgrading, aim to get the largest capacity drive you can afford. Even if you think you won't need a large amount of space today, there's a good chance you'll need the extra storage space later.

When upgrading, usually you'll want to look for the fastest specification. Currently that's Ultra DMA/100 mode, which provides a fast data transfer rate of 100Mb/second. Ultra DMA/66 may soon become dated.

Dell hard drive

The average storage capacity of a hard drive is now about 30Gb-40Gb and most should now support the newer Ultra DMA ATA/100 high speed interface.

Usually, try to opt for the largest capacity hard drive you can afford. For a desktop PC today, aim for a minimum of 30Gb – you may not need this amount of space today, but it's amazing how quickly today's hard drives can fill up, especially when you consider the sizes of music and video clips alone.

Getting ready to upgrade

There are several important things to consider when thinking about buying a drive. The most obvious reason to consider upgrading to another hard drive is to make more storage space available to your PC. Other reasons include replacing a slower drive with one of the new breed of fast drives, or simply replacing a broken hard drive.

However, sometimes upgrading may not be as straightforward as we might think. Read your PC's user guide or speak to your supplier, to find out your options for upgrading your existing hard drive or adding another. Why? You may be limited to a specific type of hard drive.

Hard drive specifications

Three main features help determine how a hard drive will perform: **cost**, **reliability** and **speed**. During the last few years, while costs have come down, reliability has generally improved: check out what is available from proven makers like Western Digital, Maxtor, Fujitsu, Seagate and IBM. More about speed in a moment. Hard drives have several essential specifications that are essential to consider before buying, including:

- Drive type: do you want SCSI or E-IDE?

- Drive capacity: measured in millions of bytes

- Physical size: usually 2", 2.5" or 3.5" diameter

- Average seek time: measured in milliseconds (ms): now typically 5-12ms: the lower the better

Handle hard drives gently – they contain many sensitive components. Don't place a hard drive down heavily on any hard surface.

- Data transfer rate: measured in Mb/sec, typically 16Mb/sec or 66Mb/sec using Ultra DMA, or greater

The speed of a hard drive is the feature that interests many people and it can be determined in two main ways: by examining (1) the average seek time and (2) the transfer rate, which is measured in Mb/sec. The higher the transfer rate, the better the drive. The data transfer rate value is probably the most important measure of a drive's performance!

Three simple steps to help you choose the right drive

While fitting a drive, ideally use an antistatic mat on which to place it. Remember to power off and disconnect the power lead before starting.

1 Identify which hard drive interface you're going to use: SCSI or E-IDE.

2 Decide how much hard drive space you're going to need.

3 Decide which make and model of hard drive to purchase.

What to consider when installing a second drive

1. IDE hard drives come in several modes. Drives of mode 4 are faster than those of mode 3. When fitting a second hard drive, don't mix drives of different modes on the same controller cable, otherwise the faster hard drive may run at the slower mode of the two.

2. In a two-drive system, aim to put the new drive on the primary channel and your old drive on the secondary

channel. Why: some controllers may force the new faster drive to run at the slower speed of the old drive.

3.   To get the best out of E-IDE drives, match the disk controller with the hard drive and operating system you're going to use. Why: your controller can then support the highest mode your intended hard disk can use.

IBM 48Gb TravelStar hard drive

4.   If your PC has an older BIOS, it may not accept a hard drive larger than 528Mb. Check with your supplier before buying, to ensure that the new drive you want will function correctly.

5.   When you install your new, faster hard drive, to gain maximum benefits, you could make it your primary master drive and transfer the operating system to it. But if you're not confident about how to do this, don't. Alternatively, discuss this option with your dealer.

Just like a PC, to upgrade a hard drive, you don't need to know how it works, just the steps you need to take and enough background information to enable you to complete the necessary steps.

Not all IDE drives are compatible with each other on a single channel. Check with your supplier if you're buying a second hard drive, to ensure your choice will be compatible with your system.

The Iomega Peerless portable storage solution

If you want the convenience of simply taking the hard drive on which you're working or which contains the information you want, where you want, Iomega have just announced what might provide an ideal solution and which looks set to become a favourite portable storage solution for many users.

Here's why: the Iomega 10Gb or 20Gb portable hard drive can transfer data at speeds of up to 15Mb each second, yet is small enough to fit in a jacket pocket. You can connect the drive to a PC in a range of ways including USB sockets, Firewire, or SCSI, which just about covers most PCs around today.

Installing an E-IDE hard drive

Installing a hard drive usually requires five steps:

1 Setting up the drive: master/slave or setting SCSI ID number (covered on pages 50–53).

2 Physically installing and securing your drive. A hard drive usually installs in a space known as a drive bay.

3 Telling the PC and BIOS about your new hard drive. (Most BIOSes nowadays detect a new hard drive automatically. However, you still may need to make fine adjustments manually).

4 Partitioning the drive (covered on pages 55–57).

5 High-level formatting the new drive (page 58).

Before removing the old boot (C:) drive, make sure you've backed up all of your existing data; ideally make two copies and store them in separate locations. At the very least, back up essential or important files.

Make sure that you have all the correct screws, etc., you need. Some suppliers sell upgrade kits: ideal if you're fitting a second hard drive that doesn't come with any mounting screws. Have the small hand tools you may need available: screwdrivers, small needle-nose pliers or tweezers (to reset jumpers if necessary), plus your PC's user guide; a DOS or Windows system diskette/CD-ROM; and the new hard drive's installation guide – do read it before starting.

Installing a new hard drive

Disconnect the PC from the mains supply and remove the outer case. To remove the old C: drive, as well as unplugging its power and IDE connectors, you may have to disconnect a ground wire too.

You may also need mounting rails similar to those shown here, or other attachments necessary to install the new drive: make sure you have all the correct screws for these too.

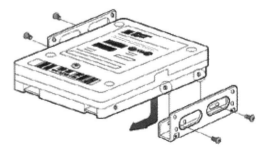

Installing a new boot drive

On the new drive, you may need to change the position of jumper links to configure the new drive as a Primary Master drive, or as a Secondary Master drive. Then install the new drive carefully into the casing, as directed by your drive installation guide.

Adding a second hard drive

Assuming your original boot drive has already been set up as the Primary Master drive, if you're adding a second hard drive, you'll need to configure the new drive either as a Primary Slave, Secondary Master or Secondary Slave. Usually, you do this by moving small jumpers on the drive assembly to link the appropriate pins. Your hard drive installation guide should provide the exact details.

Attaching the leads

Connect one end of the 40-pin flat ribbon-type interface lead to the socket on the hard drive, ensuring pin 1 on the lead aligns with pin 1 on the hard drive socket. Usually, pin 1 is the end nearest the power connector, or pin 1 may be indicated by a coloured stripe along the edge of the lead.

When fitting a hard drive, always try to ensure you use the correct mounting screws. Otherwise, if the screws you use are too long, it's possible to puncture the seal, damage the drive and also void the warranty.

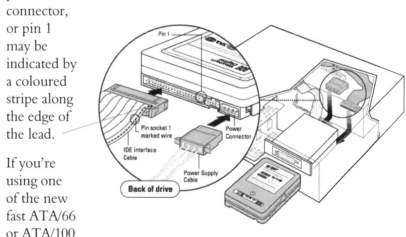

Pin 1

Pin socket 1 marked wire

IDE Interface Cable

Power Connector

Power Supply Cable

Back of drive

If you're using one of the new fast ATA/66 or ATA/100 drives that use Cable Select, this flat ribbon cable will have 80 wires instead of the old 40. Then connect the other end of the ribbon cable to the appropriate motherboard connection on the motherboard (the Primary or Secondary IDE connector) or more rarely on the IDE interface card.

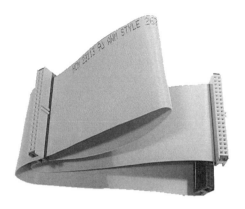

A typical 80-pin Ultra DMA hard drive connecting cable

The IDE cable is the flat 40-pin or 80-pin lead that connects your drive to the drive controller circuitry – now usually on the motherboard. To avoid signal problems, make sure the lead is not too long. Key point: use the correct lead that comes with your new hard drive, or don't use a lead longer than 46cm.

Next, connect the power connector to the hard drive: this is designed to fit in only one way, so don't force it. If your PC does not have any spare power connectors, you can purchase a Y-shaped cable adaptor/splitter from computer parts suppliers to provide the extra required power lead.

Making sense of 'Cable Select'
Many PCs nowadays identify different drives using a system called Cable Select instead of Master/Slave jumpers. If your PC uses this feature, configure the jumper links as shown in your installation guide.

Updating the BIOS
Once the drive is physically installed, when you power up again, ensure that the BIOS updates to identify the new drive. If not, you will have to update it manually (see page 60).

Partitioning, reformatting and installing files
Next, partition and format the new drive as outlined on pages 55–59. You can then finish by installing an operating system, for example: Windows 98, Me, XP, NT or 2000 onto your new boot drive. Once a hard drive is fully formatted and contains an operating system, you can install, copy and restore any application files and data to the drive.

Fitting an internal SCSI hard drive

The Small Computer Systems Interface (SCSI) provides a very high speed bus onto which you can connect various devices (peripherals) to a motherboard. For example: CD-ROM and tape drives, graphics scanners and hard drives.

To attach a SCSI hard drive, we need a SCSI interface. Some modern motherboards now come with this built in. On others, you need a special plug-in card called a host adaptor. The host adaptor essentially acts like a bridge from the SCSI bus to the motherboard's system bus.

Advanced Storage Concepts
PCI SCSI host adaptor card

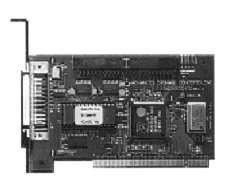

The Fast and Wide version of the SCSI-2 standard can transfer data at 20M/sec. The more recent SCSI-3 Ultra standards provide up to 40M/sec, 80M/sec and even 160M/sec versions of SCSI-3 standard.

Consequently, SCSI tends to be used in PC systems where speed is especially important, or where there is a need to connect more than four devices to the PC. However, this improved performance is reflected in SCSI hard drive prices, which tend to be higher than their E-IDE equivalents.

The SCSI host adapter card

To install a SCSI hard drive, unless you have a motherboard containing a built-in SCSI interface, you'll also need a SCSI host adapter card, and this counts as one of the number of devices you can connect together in a daisy-chain sequence.

Setting up a SCSI hard drive

You can link up to 7 or 15 devices – including hard drives – in a SCSI chain, and you don't need to configure the master/slave jumpers. However, each device/drive must be given an identification (ID) number between 0 and 15. Usually the highest priority or ID number (7 or 15) is reserved for the host adapter card and the lowest (0) for the SCSI itself.

Although you can have up to 15 devices (16 really, but one device is actually the host adaptor card) attached to a single SCSI host adaptor, most modern motherboards can handle up to 4 host adaptors, providing a maximum of up to 60 devices if you're really looking for adventure! Furthermore, the latest double channel adaptors can even double the maximum again!

High capacity hard drive from Fujitsu

You can usually set the ID by setting up jumpers on each drive, or moving an adjuster switch or dial to read the correct ID. Carry out the instructions provided in the drive's user guide.

Installing and terminating a SCSI drive

The procedure for physical installation is similar to that of an E-IDE drive as described on pages 49–51, except that SCSI usually uses a 50-pin connector.

After installing the drive, however, you must also set up the termination status correctly, using the correct terminators. Optionally, several other adjustments may also be needed. Again, refer to your particular SCSI guide for details, as each situation may require a different setup procedure.

Installing a hard drive in a notebook PC

Notebook PCs seem to have a habit of never having enough hard drive space, so there may come a time when you want to upgrade the hard drive. Nowadays, the task may be easier than you might at first think, especially if your notebook is a well-known brand which contains a removable hard drive or uses a removable caddy system. You simply contact your approved supplier, purchase the upgrade and swap the drives, according to the supplied instructions.

PC Cards come in three types: Type I (3.3mm thick), Type II (5mm) and Type III (10.5mm). Physically, the main difference is thickness: hard drives typically use Type III.

If it's not possible to upgrade the hard drive in a notebook, you may be able to use a plug-in PC Card (PCMCIA) hard drive. However, check compatibility issues with your notebook supplier first (see the Hot Tips in the margin).

TravelMate 730 from ACER

PC Cards are backward-compatible, so a Type I or Type II PC Card can fit into a Type III slot, or a Type I into a Type II slot. However, a Type III PC Card won't fit into a Type I or Type II slot.

Upgrading older notebook hard drives

If the hard drive is not a 'removable' type, you'll need to examine your options in more detail. First, establish for certain – ideally with the manufacturers or their representatives – *whether your notebook can be upgraded and whether it is cost-effective to do so*. Then, after obtaining the correct 2" or 2.5" (or more rarely 3.5") drive, you're ready to complete the task.

If the drive comes with instructions, follow those carefully. Caution: notebooks can sometimes be harder to dismantle than their desktop cousins, but take your time and perform each step carefully and correctly before continuing.

Confirming BIOS updates

As a final step, you might have to update the PC's SETUP BIOS with the changes you've made. If the new hard drive is a larger size, but your notebook PC is somewhat older you may need to use a special program to enable the PC to recognise the full size of the hard drive. Several types of these programs are available, including: *EZ-Drive*, *Disk Manager* from Seagate and Ontrack, and the *MaxBlast* utility from Maxtor.

Partitioning a hard drive

Preparing to partition – an overview

A completely new hard drive must be prepared in three stages: (1) the drive must be **low-level formatted**, (2) it must be **partitioned**, and finally (3) it must be **high-level formatted.**

Low level formatting creates the basic low-level framework on which the data is stored. Usually, new hard drives are low-level formatted by the makers.

Normally, if you change the partition size on a hard drive, you'll destroy all the data. However, by using a tool such as PartitionMagic from PowerQuest, you can change partitions 'on the fly' without deleting any data.

Introduction to partitioning

Two levels of partition are available for the FAT system: **primary** and **extended**. All drives must have at least one (primary) partition. An extended partition can be created to split a large drive into smaller more manageable chunks termed logical drives. Up to 25 logical drives can be created in this way.

However, nowadays, you can create more efficient use of disk space having only one or two large partitions – preferably only one called drive C:. Each additional partition can then be identified as a separate drive letter, like D:, E:, and so on.

WARNING: IN A MULTI-DRIVE SYSTEM, BE CAREFUL NOT TO PARTITION A DRIVE CONTAINING DATA YOU WANT TO KEEP. IF YOU GET THIS WRONG, YOU MAY ERASE REQUIRED DATA PERMANENTLY, <u>AND PERMANENT DELETION ONLY TAKES SECONDS!</u>

In earlier versions of Windows, the older FAT16 DOS system allowed for partitions up to 2.1Gb. With the newer FAT32 system however, partitions of up to 2,048Gb are possible. Windows NT and 2000 use the NTFS file system which allows for a maximum partition size of 16 exabytes (an absolutely incredible size: 10^{18} bytes).

Partitioning a new hard drive

You can partition a hard drive using proprietary software that may come with your hard disk, or you can use the FDISK command that comes with your operating system. Ideally, use FDISK as it represents a true standard (page 56).

Proprietary software like Ontrack's *Disk Manager* or Maxtor's *MaxBlast* present a more user-friendly face. However, read the documentation that comes with your drive and then you can decide how you want to partition your new drive.

Using FDISK: CAUTION

FDISK.EXE is a powerful utility supplied with Microsoft Windows that allows you to set up a primary DOS partition and extended DOS partitions with logical drives. FDISK will completely wipe a hard drive, erasing all information. Key guideline: understand how to use the program before use.

Computer Step or the author cannot accept any responsibility for any damage incurred as a result of using FDISK. Having mentioned the legal stuff, the reason why FDISK is so dangerous to your data is that it doesn't provide many 'loud' warnings before wiping a disk.

Often, other programs which perform the same job provide excellent online help to guide you through the process. FDISK, however, was originally supplied as part of the MS-DOS operating system since DOS version 3.3 and so is a tried and tested utility.

The outline procedures on these pages are for guidance purposes only: for the exact procedure for your drive system, refer to your operating system's documentation or your new drive's documentation. Use FDISK with great care and caution.

Primary and extended partitions and logical drives

A primary partition contains the essential files necessary to load your operating system when you start your PC. All DOS-based PCs – including those that use Windows 95, 98, Me, and XP and those that use the Windows 2000 native NTFS system – must have a primary partition.

As FDISK is a powerful utility that can completely wipe a hard drive with a few keystrokes, I strongly recommend you keep this utility on a floppy disk, Zip disk, or other external source. Save FDISK.EXE on your hard drive only when you want to use it, then remove after use.

An extended partition is space on a hard drive where you can store your applications and data only, if you wish, keeping the operating system on the primary partition. Extended partitions are not essential. A logical drive – also known as a volume – is space within an extended partition to which you can designate a drive number, for example, drive E:. You can establish up to 23 logical drives using this method.

Partitioning a primary drive using FDISK.EXE

The following guidelines apply to a hard drive which has been set as the master drive on a primary IDE connector. Some hard drive suppliers include their own floppy disk containing FDISK. If not, you'll need to have a disk containing FDISK.EXE and FORMAT.COM (for your particular operating system) ready to use.

Partitioning guidelines using FDISK.EXE

1 Insert a DOS/Windows system diskette/bootable floppy diskette into the floppy drive and restart the PC.

2 When you see the DOS prompt, insert a DOS/Windows diskette containing FDISK.EXE and FORMAT.COM.

3 At the A: prompt, type: FDISK then press the Enter key. A screen display similar to that below appears.

If you've installed a second drive, you must usually choose option 5 first. Then in the following screen display, FDISK recognises the new drive as Disk 2 in a two-drive system. So you would type 2, then press Enter to return to the FDISK options screen shown here.

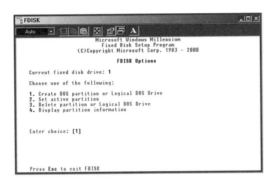

4 If you have two hard drives, five options are displayed. The fifth option lets you specify which disk to partition. MAKE SURE THE DRIVE YOU WANT TO PARTITION IS CHOSEN.

Some of the steps outlined on this page may vary in results, depending on the particular version of DOS/Windows you're using.

5 Choose the option for 'Create DOS partition or Logical DOS Drive', by pressing 1, then press Enter.

6 FDISK displays a message asking if you want to make the primary DOS partition the maximum size possible or a smaller size. If you choose not to use the maximum space, you must create an extended DOS partition to make full use of the drive space. Next, choose the option for 'Create Primary DOS Partition', by pressing 1, then press Enter.

7 Choose the option to make the primary DOS partition active.

8 When partitioning is complete, exit from FDISK. Now format the drive using the FORMAT.COM command overleaf.

Formatting a hard drive

Formatting, in this sense, refers to the action of high-level formatting a hard drive, which prepares a drive to receive data. It can be likened to putting the guidelines lines on writing paper. *Warning: formatting a drive destroys all existing data on the drive.* Windows uses the command FORMAT.COM to format a hard drive. To format a drive using FORMAT.COM, perform the following steps.

1 After partitioning using FDISK, make sure the disk containing FORMAT.COM is in the floppy drive. Next, type FORMAT C: where C: represents the drive you've just partitioned (in this example, we've chosen the C: drive). Then press the Enter key.

If the newly formatted drive is to be your primary hard drive, you must install an operating system on the drive to use it. If the drive is not your primary drive, you can install any desired data and applications, or restore any backed-up data.

2 FORMAT.COM then asks if you want to continue. Remember, formatting erases all data off the target drive. Press the Y key if you want to continue.

3 After the hard drive is formatted, FORMAT.COM may ask you to type a label for the hard drive. This is optional; type a label and press Enter, or simply press Enter to complete the formatting process: you should then see the 'DOS prompt' – normally shown as C:\. Now, you're ready to install your operating system. Check your documentation for precise instructions.

CAUTION: You can also run FORMAT.COM from Windows Explorer, so take care later not to accidentally run this program unintentionally.

Using overlay software

If the BIOS in a PC will not accept a hard drive larger than 528Mb, one option is to use special overlay software such as *EZ-Drive* or Ontrack *Disk Manager*.

Overlay software alters the master boot record on a hard drive to ensure a special driver is loaded before the operating system accesses the drive. The overlay software rather than the BIOS then controls disk access.

However, overlay software should not be used as a simple alternative to using proper partitioning and formatting software like FDISK.EXE and FORMAT.COM and is less likely to be needed nowadays anyway.

Data Recovery • Software • Services
Datenrettung • Software • Dienste
Récupération de données • Logiciels • Services
Recuperación de datos • Software • Servicios

After installing the operating system, it's a good time perhaps to reconsider your directory layout, to minimise the number of sub-directories immediately below the root directory.

It's probably better to use overlay software only if you have no other choice. If, for example, your PC BIOS supports LBA (Logical Block Addressing) and large hard drives of, say, over 2Gb, then there should be no need to use overlay software.

Updating the BIOS and finishing off

After installing a hard drive, the PC's BIOS setup program must be updated to match the characteristics of the new hard drive. When you first switch on after installing a new hard drive in an older PC, you may see an error message referring to the new drive: this is usual until you have updated the BIOS correctly.

However, in most recently-manufactured PCs, the BIOS may automatically recognise the new drive. Don't assume this to be the case, though: always confirm the BIOS has the correct information, otherwise the PC will not be able to recognise the new drive properly. Follow the instructions that came with your new drive to update your BIOS.

If your system doesn't appear to recognise the new hard drive, one possible cause could be an incorrectly aligned IDE connector lead. Make sure pin 1 on the lead (usually shown with a coloured stripe) connects to pin 1 on the socket.

Upgrading the BIOS

Some older PCs won't normally let you access hard drives larger than 528Mb. You could get around this problem by using overlay software, as described on page 59. Alternatively, you may be able to get a BIOS chip upgrade, or you may be able to plug in a special adaptor card. AMI have produced an adaptor card which appears to work with most BIOS chips, but check with your supplier to ensure full compatibility.

A PC's BIOS SETUP program may be referred to as the CMOS setup in some user guides/ PCs. CMOS simply refers to the type of IC that is used to hold the data.

Completing your hard drive installation

Once you've installed the new hard drive, partitioned and formatted it, you are ready to finish off. Make sure all the internal connections are complete and carefully refit the case, making sure no interconnecting wires are trapped. Switch on the PC and make sure you either see the prompt like D:\ where D represents the letter assigned to your boot drive (normally C:\), or that your system starts normally. If you don't see the prompt when you should, retrace all your steps in the supplied documentation and if necessary contact your drive's supplier for advice.

If the drive installed is to become the boot drive, you can now install an extended operating system and any desired applications. If the drive is a second drive, you can simply install any desired applications, or restore or copy any desired data to the drive. Congratulations!

Maintaining a hard drive

It's a common misconception that a hard drive will look after itself, or that there's nothing you can possibly do to extend its life. In this chapter, we examine ways in which you can easily maintain and extend the life of your hard drive(s).

Covers

Chapter Six

Hints and tips on using hard drives

Today's hard drives are amazing examples of modern engineering. However, like any complex structure, they can be susceptible to certain problems. Also, there are simple procedures that you can perform to extend the life of any hard drive. Consider the following guidelines:

- Don't move a PC while it is switched on. Hard drives are most vulnerable at this stage and can easily be damaged by abrupt physical movement or jolting.

- When installing additional hard drives, try to ensure there is an adequate air space between adjacent drives: this helps maximise the rate of air flow and ensures that the drives are cooled sufficiently.

- Make sure your existing hard drives – and any new hard drives you buy – include automatic hard drive parking when the PC is switched off. If not, install and use a suitable hard drive parking program.

- To maximise the efficiency of a hard drive, regularly perform defragmenting routines. In Windows, you can use the Disk Defragmenter utility to defragment your drives. Defragmentation is explained on page 64.

- Don't place a PC in direct strong sunlight or near to any strong heat sources, such as heating radiators. Too much heat can overload the cooling circuitry.

- In a multiple-drive system, on any single channel, always try to ensure that the faster hard drive is set up as the master and the slower drive as a slave device.

- Treat an uninstalled hard drive with particular care: avoid knocking or bumping.

- To make full use of your total hard drive capacity, make sure all your hard drives are partitioned and formatted to use their full capacity. Some new drives are set up to use only two-thirds of their available storage space, simply because it can save preparation time for the maker or supplier!

Using Microsoft Windows ScanDisk

Your hard drive is divided into logical areas known as 'clusters', in which small pieces of data are stored. When saving a file to the hard drive, your operating system simply looks for the next available space, which can be anywhere on the drive. If a file won't fit into the current group of clusters, it is split up, and so may be distributed across several regions of the disk.

Fragmented clusters are linked with 'pointers', which tell the operating system which cluster should be accessed next in order to save or read a particular file. If an error occurs and a pointer points to the wrong cluster, a file may become unusable. ScanDisk examines these pointers, and tries to fix any errors, checks the physical surface of the disk, and can mark off damaged clusters as 'bad', to avoid using later.

In Windows 98, Me, XP, NT and 2000, although you can run ScanDisk whenever you want, you can also set up Windows to run ScanDisk automatically. See your Windows documentation.

1 In Windows 95, 98, Me and XP, click the Start button, followed by Programs>Accessories>System Tools>ScanDisk.

2 When the ScanDisk dialog box appears, click the drive you want to scan to highlight it.

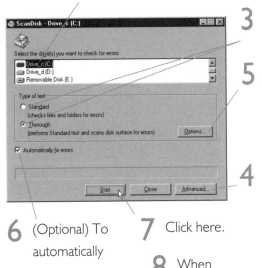

3 Click the Standard or Thorough scan option.

5 If you chose 'Thorough', you can change the settings ScanDisk uses by clicking Options.

4 If you chose 'Standard', you can change the way ScanDisk performs checks by clicking Advanced.

6 (Optional) To automatically correct any errors, click here.

7 Click here.

8 When complete, click Close.

Defragmenting your hard drive

During normal usage, files can fragment into different locations on your hard drive. The Disk Defragmenter utility helps keep your files in an orderly, logical pattern by rearranging files so that they are stored in contiguous locations. If a hard drive is badly defragmented, running Disk Defragmenter can actually speed up performance. To defragment a drive, carry out the following steps.

1 In Windows 95, 98, Me and XP, click the Start button, followed by Programs>Accessories>System Tools>Disk Defragmenter.

2 Click the drive you want to defragment. If you want to defragment all drives, click the All Hard Drives option.

If you use your PC daily, ideally check whether your PC needs defragmenting at least once a month using Disk Defragmenter. Windows 2000 Defragmenter can also check and advise whether defragmenting is required.

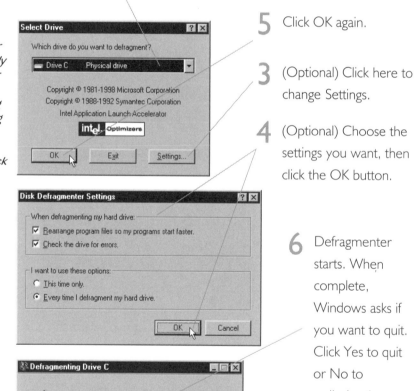

5 Click OK again.

3 (Optional) Click here to change Settings.

4 (Optional) Choose the settings you want, then click the OK button.

6 Defragmenter starts. When complete, Windows asks if you want to quit. Click Yes to quit or No to redisplay the Select Drive dialog box.

Safeguarding your data

What price do you put on your data? What would happen if you lost it all tomorrow? With information now becoming the real currency of today, the data stored on your PC can become worth much more than the PC itself! For business users, this data is often crucial for commercial survival. In this chapter, we examine why it is so important to back up data regularly, and look at the most important aspects of backing up.

Covers

Chapter Seven

Establishing a backup strategy

Computer data can become damaged in many ways, including: electrical spikes; lightning strikes; worn hard drives; computer viruses; and of course PC theft. Although PCs can be replaced easily, often the data is unique and irreplaceable. If data is important to you and time is money, a detailed regular backup solution set up to run automatically is essential, not optional.

For backup of individual files, the LS120 drives – that can also read the old 1.44Mb floppy disks – are currently the most popular choice of removable media. However, for complete PC system backup, a range of tape- and disk-based backup options are available, as discussed in the following pages. Then once your daily or weekly backup system is set up and established, you can simply follow your procedure and spend time using your PC in more interesting ways.

Develop a backup system that works for you, and make sure you have more than one copy of each data backup. It's also a good idea to keep a simple written log of your backups.

Once you get in the backup habit, you can adjust your work around the time when you know you need to back up – or you may prefer to simply back up your data overnight, or when you're not using your PC. The absolutely crucial point is not which device you choose to make the backups, but rather when and how you actually perform your backups.

The only way to minimise data loss is to back up regularly, and increase the number and frequency of backups if you're working on especially sensitive data.

Devise a backup system that works for you

A simple option: simply back up your PC once a week to one disk or tape. However, this approach has obvious gaps. A better solution would be to use several disks or tapes. For example, you could back up the entire hard drive to multiple disks/tapes, or you could make sure you place all your data on one drive or location – for example: 'My Documents' in Microsoft Windows – and just back up your data. This option is quicker and uses fewer disks or tapes, whereas a backup of the full hard drive is simpler, more thorough and can be scheduled to run overnight if desired.

Most important: work out a simple system that ensures all data is backed up and that you always have at least two backup copies. Also, ideally, keep at least one backup set in a different location to ensure against fire, flood, or other unexpected events.

Choosing a backup device

Introducing backup options

To recap, all computer backup options can be grouped into two main categories: tape or disk. Tape uses a sequential method of backup, so that data block A must be backed up before data block B, and so on. Disk backup, however, is random and so multiple blocks can be backed up apparently simultaneously. Therefore, disk backup is much faster than tape, so is generally more expensive.

Tape-based backup solutions

Defragment your hard drive regularly, so that ideally, your data is defragmented before being backed up. Windows comes with its own Disk Defragmenter tool, accessible from the Start button.

Currently, tape backup is available in several formats:

- **Travan:** QIC-based systems – which include the popular Travan range and the QIC-wide formats – use linear tape transport in which the tape moves sequentially past a fixed read/write head. The Travan TR-4, based on the QIC-3095 standard, can backup up to 4Gb of uncompressed data and 8Gb using 2:1 compression. The Travan Network Series NS-20 can store up to 20Gb using a 2:1 compression ratio.

To reduce the time needed to complete a backup, you could rearrange the data on your PC: e.g., place the operating system on drive C and your data on drive D. Also, set up your backup software to exclude certain arguably unnecessary files, like .TMP and .BAK files.

- **Digital Audio Tape (DAT):** the DAT system wraps the tape around a rotating read/write head in a helical fashion. The QIC-5B DC Data cartridge can back up an amazing 5Gb of data, whereas the best current DDS-4 DAT drives can hold up to 40Gb or more on a single DAT cartridge.

- **Advanced Digital Recording (ADR):** the latest ADR system from OnStream can store up to an amazing 50Gb using 2:1 compression ratio on a single tape.

- **Digital Linear Tape (DLT):** usually a more expensive but equally durable system, DLT can back up 70Gb on a single DLT 7000 tape at a fast 1-10Mb/sec using 2:1 compression.

Disk-based backup solutions

Disk-based backup options include: using a second hard drive, the Iomega Zip and Jaz removable disks, and recordable CD/DVD-ROMs. However, most disk-based options may not be able to fit say the contents of an 8Gb hard drive onto a single disk – so someone has to be available to change disks. Although recordable DVD disks look promising, at the time of writing, the technology is still evolving. For backup purposes, where you need a highly reliable medium, existing established tape backup systems are probably a safer option – for now at least.

Deciding whether to opt for tape or disk

Although smaller data files can be backed up to the latest 120Mb floppy disks and larger chunks of data to an Iomega Jaz disk for example, if you want a complete backup solution with minimal interference to your daily work routine, you might want to opt for a tape-based system that can fit all that you want to back up onto a single tape.

If you want to save money, then a tape-based system may also suit your needs better: tapes are usually cheaper than disks. A typical Digital Audio Tape (DAT) or Travan tape system can store 8Gb onto one low-priced tape without any intervention. Internal tape drives are also usually the cheapest option.

However, external drives are ideal if you want to back up more than one PC, are essential if you don't have a spare drive bay in your PC, and may be ideal for notebooks as hard drive sizes tend to be smaller than their desktop cousins. If you want to backup more quickly, then a more expensive disk-based system may be more appropriate.

Before backing up, shut down any programs you're not using. Why? Microsoft Windows, for example, usually will not back up any open files. However, you may be able to set up the backup software to retry backing up open files later. Alternatively, close down all files and back up everything in one session.

If you're looking to save money, the 8Gb Travan-based options may provide the cheapest backup solution. Nevertheless, do compare prices for drive purchase and running costs.

Tape backup interface card

Internal tape backup unit

Example backup tape

CD ReWriteable drives

Currently, CD-ROM drives are available in three main types, those on which we can:

- Read (play) but not write (record) over data: like standard audio CDs, software application CDs, etc.

- Write information once only, and read many times – Write Once Read Many (WORM) devices: these are the most common writeable CD-ROM drives to-date and are often referred to as using CD-R or CD-Recordable technology. A successfully recorded CD-R disk can be read by any standard CD-ROM drive.

- Write information to many times – currently this new CD-RW standard suggests that these devices can be successfully re-written to about 1000 times!

Backup drives that use an optical system don't usually provide the fast retrieval speeds of hard disk-based systems, and can be quite expensive. However, optical backup cartridges may be cheaper when bought in quantities.

Why use writeable CD-ROMs?

Writeable CD-ROM disks can provide an ideal low cost data storage or archival solution. Here's why:

CD-ROM drive speeds seem to be increasing as new technology develops: CD-RW drives now typically write (record) at 12x-speed to 16x-speed, while reading at 10x-speed, although some can currently reach up to 40x normal speed.

- With each disk able to store around 650Mb of data, some people consider using recordable CD-ROM disks as the ideal backbone for a backup system.

- Recordable CD-ROMs are ideal if the data you want to back up is unlikely to change – such as archive material – since data written to a WORM CD-ROM disk cannot be deleted once it has been created.

- Also, rewriteable CD-ROMs are now quite cheap compared to magnetic media equivalents – CD-RW drives currently cost around £100-£250 or less, while disks often cost less than £2 each. For Windows 98/Me/XP/2000 users, a PC with USB v2.0 using a USB-based CD-RW drive provides an excellent backup solution.

- The recorded data is not affected by any electromagnetic interference and has a much longer storage life than magnetic tapes, disks, etc.

The Iomega Jaz drive

If you want to backup your PC fast and are prepared to pay the extra cost, the Iomega Jaz drive could solve your backup problem at a stroke!

The Jaz drive is essentially a hard drive housing into which you insert a 2Gb removable hard disk, onto which you back up your data. If you need more storage, you simply remove the full disk and insert the next disk when prompted, until the backup is finished.

Removable storage devices, like the Iomega Jaz drive, can provide fast data backup at a cost that may be considered sustainable in relation to time taken.

If you want to fit an internal Jaz drive, but only have a spare 5.25" drive bay, adaptor kits are usually available to house a 3.5" Jaz drive. For more details, contact your computer supplier.

Iomega Jaz drive and Jaz disks

However, 2Gb disks can't be used in the older, now discontinued 1Gb Jaz drive: otherwise damage may result to both drive and media. However, 3:1 and 2:1 compression is available, so it's possible to backup around 4Gb using a 2Gb cartridge.

The magic moment is when you realise 1Gb can be backed up in about six minutes. Compare that to several hours with a Travan tape system when the data is backed up and also compared.

The Jaz drive requires a SCSI controller interface card to make the connection to the motherboard. However, usually this is not supplied. The Jaz drive is available as an external model or as an internal unit that fits into a 3.5" or 5.25" floppy drive bay, and drivers are available for DOS and Windows. The main drawback with a Jaz drive is the price of the removable drive cartridges: at the time of writing about £70 for a 2Gb disk; if you buy them in packs of three, you can generally save money.

The Iomega Zip drive

The Iomega Zip drive is now a well established format. About the same size as a 3.5" floppy drive, the Zip accepts special rigid disks that are thicker than a floppy disk and which can store 100Mb-250Mb of data.

The latest 250Mb version can also read the older 100Mb disks and offers some exciting possibilities. Perhaps even a 500Mb disk – or larger – may follow within a year or so? The Zip drive is available as an internal model: SCSI or IDE, or as an external model, in SCSI, parallel port and Universal Serial Bus (USB) versions.

Some users of early Zip and Jaz drives have been reporting some problems after a specific time. When a drive is afflicted with an unusual series of clicks, this may indicate a problem is about to happen. If it does occur, you could lose your entire data on that particular zip disk. Contact Iomega for advice and great technical support.

Iomega Zip drive and Zip disks

The Zip drive is ideal for many people in that it combines the benefits of a hard drive with those of a removable cartridge. An access time of about 29ms or better, plus the 1Mb transfer rate when used with a SCSI interface can make the drive a worthy addition to your PC. However, the SCSI version generally has the fastest overall response. Impressive to say the least!

Iomega also recently released the physically small 'Clik' series of removable media drives with storage capacities of up to 40Mb. Clik is designed to be used with notebook PCs and digital cameras.

The 'standard' external version plugs into the PC's parallel (printer) port, whereas the external USB version is probably the easiest to set up provided your PC has a USB port – fortunately, most PCs now include at least 2 USB ports.

However, some early Zip drives developed a problem known as 'Click of Death', which refers to a sudden unusual clicking sound developing in the drive, that may result in both drive and disk being damaged. More information about detection and remedies are available at: www.iomega.com/ and the superb Gibson Research site at: www.grc.com/

Other removable drive options

Removable storage drives essentially use one of two technologies:

- Optical: like the magneto-optical drives. Generally, the recording media is considerably cheaper than the equivalent magnetic media, hence why this technology represents a popular backup medium. However, access time is usually slower – around 30ms – compare that to an average 10ms, or less, for a typical modern hard drive.

- Magnetic: see below and previous sections on the Iomega Zip and Jaz drives.

Optical and Magneto-Optical (MO) drives

An optical read-write device can provide the benefits of CDs, fast backup speed, and the use of non-magnetic media for durable, long-life storage. Today's largest MO drives can back up over 5Gb to a single disk.

The prices of optical media are also much more competitive now than previously. Magneto-Optical drives are often available in a range of forms: for example: IDE, SCSI, USB and FireWire, though the fast SCSI standard tends to be the favourite.

Several notable manufacturers produce removable hard drives, and most are based on the renowned Bernoulli designs. If you consider buying one of these, check out how the drive performs compared to other backup systems available before buying.

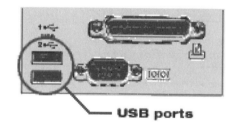

USB ports

Confirm the type of controller required – IDE, SCSI or USB – as this can add substantially to your costs (you may need a SCSI host adaptor card). Also, make sure the correct drivers are available for the operating system you're using.

Installing a tape backup unit

Installing an external tape backup unit

External tape backup units are ideal if: (1) you don't have a spare bay in which to fit an internal model, (2) you're using a notebook PC, or (3) you simply don't want to get involved in removing the PC's cover to fit an internal upgrade.

Installing an external backup unit is straightforward: you simply connect the tape unit to the parallel (printer) socket or USB connector on your PC using the supplied lead. Many models include a 'loop-through' connection so that you can then permanently connect your printer to the tape backup unit and print on demand.

Hewlett Packard Surestore
DAT 24 tape backup units
(external and internal)

Always store backup tapes well away from any magnetic sources, like telephones, loudspeakers, computer displays and so on. The magnetic fields present in these devices can ruin (scramble) a tape backup.

You then only need install the backup software and check the new unit by performing a test backup and restore.

Installing an internal tape backup unit

Backup tapes do wear out eventually. One way to even the wear and tear on tapes is to initially buy more, then simply cycle the tapes as you use them.

Often, internal tape backup units come in a support cage designed to fit into a 5.25" drive bay.

However, usually you can remove the cage if it's not required and you want to fit the tape backup unit directly into a 3.5" drive bay.

After physically installing the drive according to the maker's instructions, you'll need to connect a spare power connector lead to the drive. If no spare lead is available, you can purchase a 'splitter' cable, like the one shown overleaf, that can provide the extra power connector required.

Most QIC-based backup units are designed to connect to a spare connector on the floppy disk interface cable. If no spare connector is available, usually the supplier provides a special 'splitter' cable which you can install in place of the existing

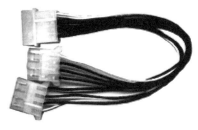

floppy disk controller lead. Make sure pin 1 on the lead aligns with pin 1 on the tape backup unit socket. Then, you're ready to install the software.

Microsoft Windows 95, 98, Me, XP, NT and 2000 include the 'Backup' utility, which supports a wide range of backup devices. For more information on your particular version, read your Windows documentation or Help file.

If you're unlucky with your choice, you may need an expansion adapter to link your tape unit to the PC. Check with your supplier. Some tape drives can connect to a SCSI controller or an E-IDE channel. If you use an E-IDE channel, if possible set the tape drive as a master on a separate channel to the hard

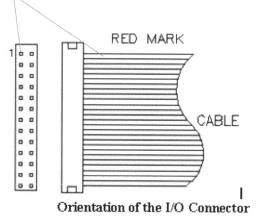

Orientation of the I/O Connector

IDE lead showing one
way of identifying pin 1

drive(s). Why? To prevent the normal operation speed of the hard drive being slowed to match the response of the new tape drive.

Make sure you install the correct backup software for your operating system and follow the installation instructions that come with your backup device or dedicated backup software.

Microsoft Windows should automatically recognize your new backup device and install the drivers for it, or prompt you to insert the disk containing the required drivers. Usually when you purchase a tape or disk backup kit, appropriate backup software is also provided by the supplier.

Other backup solutions

A range of additional backup options are now also available as described below.

Using a second hard drive to back up the main one

With this option, you can simply install a second hard drive the same size or larger than the original drive. Then create a regularly updated mirror image of the original data on the second hard drive. If needed, your backed-up copy could quickly and easily restore your original system. Drawback: a larger theft risk: data is not kept separate from the PC.

An external hard drive

If your PC has the fast USB version 2.0-compatible connectors and you're using Windows 98, Me, XP or 2000, a USB-based CD-RW drive combined with the now low cost of CD-RW disks can provide an excellent overall backup solution.

This option provides the same benefits mentioned in the previous paragraph, and also allows you to store your data in a separate location. Kits are also available to convert an internal hard drive into one which can be used externally. Discuss options with your supplier to confirm whether your second drive can be converted/matched to your existing PC.

The Iomega Peerless portable storage solution

If you want the convenient option of simply taking the hard drive on which you're working, or which contains the information you want, where you want, Iomega have just announced what might provide an ideal solution and which looks set to become a favourite portable storage solution for many users.

Here's why: the Iomega Peerless 10Gb or 20Gb portable hard drive can transfer data at speeds of up to 15Mb each second, yet is small enough to fit in a jacket pocket. You can connect the drive to a PC in a range of ways including USB sockets, Firewire, or SCSI.

DVD recordable drives

DVD-ROM drives have emerged as a new powerful record and playback medium. Although originally designed to replace video tapes, a DVD-ROM drive could also provide an effective backup solution. Amazing rapid advances in compression technology in this area promise much for the future. DVD drives deserve special attention and so are covered in depth in Chapter Thirteen.

If the mains supply fails

If the power supply fails while your PC is operational and a backup power supply of some sort is not connected to your PC, any information that you have not already saved will simply be lost.

If your data is especially valuable, considering any unusual possible threats is a worthwhile exercise. For example, lightning doesn't have to strike a PC directly to destroy it: electrical surges through the mains supply can occur during storms that can effectively destroy a PC and anything connected to it.

Also, your Windows files may become damaged by the sudden shutdown. Why: Windows requires open files to be closed properly and the operating system to be correctly shut down before a PC is switched off.

One way to avoid these risks is to connect your PC to an Uninterruptible Power Supply (UPS), which, in the event of power supply fluctuations or complete power failure,

Range of UPSs available from Merlin Gerin (IDC Systems Ltd)

provides enough backup power to finish essential tasks and close down Windows normally. Most UPSs provide about 15 minutes of power, although the more expensive devices may support longer periods. Some UPSs include alarm indicators and automatic shutdown routines too.

Lightning and storms can also affect phone land lines even if a direct strike does not occur. If you're especially concerned about your PC during a severe storm, unplug both your PC from the mains supply and unplug the phone modem connection also.

Dealing with power surges

Electrical surges and spikes on the mains supply are much more common than complete power failure. If these surges get through the power supply, they can cause serious problems on a PC. Fortunately, there is a better level of protection available in the form of a surge protector.

Surge protectors are also often included in a UPS. However, bear in mind, these devices don't completely protect your PC from damage. An unlucky lightning strike could jump across a surge protector and destroy the PC and probably anything that is electrically connected to it.

Floppy disk drives

On the PC life cycle time-scale, the standard 3.5" floppy disk drive has been around for a long time and is looking dated today. Fortunately, in recent years, a newer, much more powerful version has emerged: the SuperDisk or LS-120. Nevertheless, the original floppy drive is still with us, so in this chapter, we examine the different types of floppy drive available and learn how to fit a replacement drive in a PC.

Covers

Chapter Eight

Floppy disk drive overview

The standard 3.5" floppy disk drive has stood the test of time and survived for a surprisingly long time – in computing terms. The main specification of the floppy drive has essentially stayed the same since IBM announced their first PC containing the 3.5" floppy drive. Perhaps its simplicity and basic reliability are the main reasons for its survival. The 1.44Mb floppy disk spins at a constant speed of only 300 rpm – incredibly slow by today's standards – and its capacity is made up of only 135 tracks per inch.

While travelling through an airport, passing a PC/floppy diskettes through the X-ray machine rather than the metal detector should not usually cause any problems. Why: normally, X-rays – a form of light – cannot harm magnetic media. Metal detectors, however, do use magnetic scanning, so will almost certainly damage data contained on floppy diskettes.

Every standard floppy drive has four sensors to monitor: the disk motor, whether a disk is present, the location of track 00 on the disk, and whether a disk is write-protected.

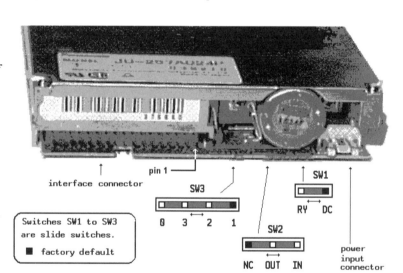

Keep all floppy disks and other types of removable media away from magnetic fields. Also avoid exposing any types of media to hot and cold temperature extremes.

Panasonic JU-257 diskette drive

The drive for ever greater storage capacity

In recent years, improvements in magnetic coatings and electronic storage systems enabled the storage density to increase. Several years ago, the 2.88Mb floppy disks – which never really became popular – enabled the data transmission rate to quadruple. Nevertheless, standard 3.5" floppy disks have essentially lost their place as the main software delivery vehicle to the CD-ROM with its much greater capacity and faster operation.

The SuperDisk

Introducing the floptical disk

The only real competition to the floppy disk has been the floptical disk. This uses optical tracking control as opposed to magnetic tracking in the floppy disk drive. Optical tracking enables a much higher number of tracks to be laid on a disk – originally allowing a storage capacity of around 20Mb on a 3.5" disk.

However, the greatest success has been the development of the SuperDisk drive outlined below.

Some years ago, several manufacturers worked together to create an entirely new, much larger capacity floppy disk format. As a result,

the LS-120 120Mb 'SuperDisk' disk format emerged. It's actually a floptical drive development – using a magnetic and optical data storage and retrieval system.

The global general public have grown to like and accept the SuperDisk. As a result, the LS120 drive is currently the most popular removeable media format, essentially replacing the 1.44Mb standard floppy disk drive in most new PCs.

The much greater storage capacity of 120Mb compared to the standard 1.44Mb (actually slightly less in practice) is – perhaps not surprisingly – causing a sensation in the computer industry!

The Imation SuperDisk drive
with PC Card connector

Ability to read 'standard' floppy disks

At the time of writing, the SuperDisk remains the latest floppy drive development using its own type of 3.5" disk format. A popular feature of the SuperDisk is that it can also read and write to standard 1.44Mb and 720Kb diskettes – and at the faster speed of 720 rpm rather than the standard floppy drive speed of 300 rpm. The later 2.88Mb floppy disks however cannot be used in a SuperDisk drive.

A rapidly emerging popular new standard

To install and use a SuperDisk drive, the BIOS in the motherboard must support the SuperDisk standard. All new motherboards should include SuperDisk coverage in their BIOS.

Unlike the Iomega Zip or Jaz drives, the SuperDisk is a new 'open' standard. So what does this really mean? Answer: various individual companies can produce their own versions under licence. Perhaps not surprisingly, take up has been enthusiastic: 3M, Imation and Matsushita (Panasonic) have all produced their own LS-120 to date, and many new PCs have the SuperDisk drive fitted as standard instead of the 'old' 1.44Mb floppy drive. What's more, you can connect a SuperDisk to your PC using any spare IDE connector.

Software support available today

Software support is available for the LS-120 in Windows 95 OSR2, Windows 98, Me, XP, NT and 2000. Unfortunately, Windows 95 standard versions did not include support as the operating system was available before this drive format was made available.

Installing a floppy disk drive

A 1.44Mb floppy drive has two main connection points to the motherboard, floppy disk controller, or I/O card. A 34-pin floppy disk cable is usually used to connect a floppy drive to the motherboard or drive controller card, for data flow. For power, a standard 4-pin keyed connector is used.

The procedure for installing a floppy disk drive depends on whether the drive is to be Drive A or Drive B. However, most users, I suspect, will be replacing a worn-out drive with a new, usually 3.5", floppy drive.

Therefore, the procedure overleaf provides a general guide for completing this task. Floppy drives also have four main settings which you may need to be aware of when installing a drive. These are: Media Sensor; Drive Select (DS) sensor; Drive Terminator; and Drive Ready sensor.

Establishing Drive A or Drive B

A standard 34-pin floppy disk cable has two connectors for connecting one or two floppy disk drives. Often, there's a twist in the cable between the Drive A and Drive B connectors.

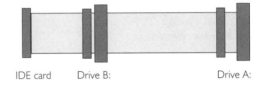

IDE card   Drive B: Drive A:

The position of each of these connectors usually determines whether a drive is Drive A or Drive B. Drive A usually connects to the connector furthest from the motherboard or disk controller IDE card.

The procedure outlined overleaf assumes the drive to be fitted is Drive A, using the furthest connector of a twisted 34-pin data cable.

If the drive you're installing is Drive B, then install the drive using the Drive B connector, and substitute the information given overleaf using the Drive B settings. If your PC doesn't use a twisted floppy drive cable, refer to your system documentation or installation sheet that comes with your new floppy drive, for information about installing and setting up your floppy drive.

1 Before you remove the existing drive, carefully note the alignment of the connectors. Next, carefully unplug the 4-pin power cable followed by the 34-pin data cable. Finally, remove the drive mounting screws and the old drive.

2 The first thing you must do is ensure the new floppy drive is configured correctly. Read the documentation that comes with your drive.

3 (Optional) If you're installing an older drive, you may need to make additional settings as outlined in the margin Beware Tip. For new drives however, these settings will almost certainly have already been completed.

Older floppy drives may have additional settings that need to be configured correctly. For example: set the Drive Select (DS) jumper to the second position: 1 if a 0/1 labelling is used, or 2 if 1/2 labelling applies. Also, if necessary, set the Disk Change (DC) jumper to the 'enabled' or 'on' position.

4 Now, install the drive carefully. Align the drive with its slot in the PC's outer casing and tighten the mounting screws.

5 Plug in the 34-pin data cable using the Drive A connector. If this connector is not keyed, align the coloured wire with pin 1 on the connector. Plug in the keyed 4-pin power connector and reassemble the PC. Congratulations!

When the PC is switched on, operating systems like Microsoft Windows automatically detect any changes made to the computer hardware and install any software drivers if required.

Expansion cards

An expansion card or Input/Output (I/O) card can easily be installed in a card slot, providing additional features to a PC. However, setting up a card to work correctly is sometimes not so straightforward. This chapter examines what you need to be aware of when installing a card, how to install a card and what action to take if problems occur.

Covers

Chapter Nine

Buses and I/O cards

An expansion card fits into an expansion slot on a motherboard. Nowadays, most motherboards include at least two types of expansion slot: PCI and AGP which connect to the PCI and AGP buses respectively.

Older motherboards may also provide the obsolete ISA slots. Some older cards often used small switches or 'jumpers' which had to be set correctly. Most PCI and AGP cards, however, are much easier to install and set up.

Never slide expansion cards across a surface. Why: static electricity may then build up which may destroy electronic components in your card.

You simply switch off the PC, remove the cover and plug the card into a suitable empty socket. Then when you switch the computer on, the Microsoft Windows (95/98/Me/XP/NT/2000) operating system should automatically detect the new card and set it up.

Input/Output (I/O) cards

An I/O card is usually only necessary if the I/O controllers are not already built in to the motherboard. Most new motherboards should at least already come with controllers for: two serial ports, a parallel port, a games port, and hard disk and floppy disk controllers. However, if you need additional I/O controllers, first check whether the additional card is compatible with your motherboard. You may have to disable some functions on a card to prevent coexistence problems.

Hold a card by the metal mounting plate and card edges – but don't touch the edge connectors. Why: to prevent any possible static electricity damage and contamination of the edge connectors. Also, while not in use, lay your cards with the component side facing downwards and store in the original packaging.

Shared ISA and PCI slots

On older motherboards containing a mix of ISA slots and PCI slots, usually the ISA slot immediately adjacent to a PCI slot shares the same location. This means you can install a card in one slot or the other, but you can't install cards in both slots at the same time. Bear this in mind if your slots are being used up and you examine your upgrade options.

An older Intel VX-series motherboard

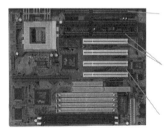

3 ISA slots

ISA and PCI slot sharing the same memory location

4 PCI slots

Installing an expansion card

Adaptor cards, I/O cards and expansion cards all require a similar handling procedure for removal and installation.

Removing adaptor cards

1 If you're removing several cards, write down a record of which card is fitted into which slot.

2 Unscrew and remove the screw holding the metal plate of each card.

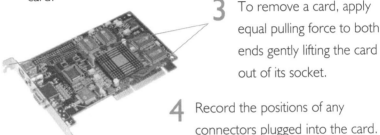

3 To remove a card, apply equal pulling force to both ends gently lifting the card out of its socket.

4 Record the positions of any connectors plugged into the card.

If a card contains dip switches, take care not to accidentally change these settings while inserting the card.

Installing adaptor cards

1 Set any jumpers or switches on the card to the correct positions as described in the card installation guide.

2 Identify the correct type of slot for the card you're installing – PCI, ISA, SCSI or AGP. Then apply equal force to align the edge connectors with the slot socket, and push down firmly but gently. Don't apply too much force as to bend the motherboard excessively.

3 Insert the card retaining screw to temporarily clamp and earth the card. Don't tighten the screw at this stage.

4 Plug any connector leads into the appropriate sockets. Make sure the connectors are aligned correctly.

5 Adjust the position of the card so the connector lead can be inserted and removed easily. Tighten the retaining screw.

Resources, conflicts and interrupts

Resources, conflicts and interrupts usually become relevant when an installation does not work properly or causes a PC to 'lock up'. Resources refer to memory addresses and special signals used on the various buses.

Conflicts occur when two or more hardware devices want to use the same resource at the same time. An interrupt or IRQ is an electronic signal sent by various hardware devices to the CPU or the chipset, asking for a request to be met.

SCSI cards/ adaptors generally use more resources than most other expansion cards (apart from sound cards usually). Also, their default settings often conflict with network cards and/or sound cards.

How do I identify a resource conflict?

Sometimes, when you install a new PC add-on, problems can occur. Often, however, the item you're installing may include some guidelines on what to do if you get problems. Unfortunately, there is no easy and simple answer here, although a basic strategy may help: see the margin Hot Tip.

Sound cards can often cause conflicts with other parts of your system. If this happens, read the documentation that came with the sound card or PC. Best advice (usually): (1) Install a video card first. (2) Leave the sound card settings in their default state and install the sound card. Ideally, let Microsoft Windows install the settings for you. (3) Change the settings in other remaining cards to resolve the conflict.

Sometimes, a resource conflict is evident when your PC will only start in Windows Safe Mode. In Microsoft Windows 95/98/Me/XP/ 2000, any conflicts are also shown highlighted in yellow or red indicators in the Device Manager available from the 'System' icon in the Windows Control Panel.

Resolving a resource conflict

1   Keep a log: note down everything you do, IN SEQUENCE.

2   Install the video card first to drive your display monitor.

3   Now, if relevant, install the sound card before any others.

4   Let Microsoft Windows arrange the resources and interrupts for any additional cards.

5   Try entering different settings. Then restart the PC repeatedly to see if a change has solved the problem.

6   Before getting too involved, contact your supplier's help-line concerning your problem: they may be able to identify it easily, saving you a lot of time and heartache.

Video cards

A video card generates the electrical signals necessary to produce images on the display monitor. Updating a video card can speed up your graphics display and provide a wider range of display modes. In this chapter, we examine the most important aspects to consider when upgrading a video card.

Covers

Chapter Ten

Video card overview

A video card creates the electrical signals that produce images on your monitor. Video cards today are much more complex than their predecessors, with video chipsets commonly dealing with many of the tasks that in previous generation cards would have been carried out by the CPU. Most cards today include several key components:

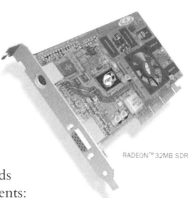

RADEON™ 32MB SDR

A video card may also be referred to as a video controller, display adapter, graphics card or graphics adaptor.

A video driver is the small software program that your operating system needs to drive your PC's video card. The correct driver is essential and updated drivers are often available from the maker's website.

- **Graphics acceleration:** includes a graphics processor with a typical core processor clock frequency of 120MHz-200MHz. Some 'high-end' cards also include additional components to handle 3D acceleration.

- **RAMDAC:** changes the video data into the kind of signals required to drive a display monitor. Current speeds are typically 300MHz-350MHz.

- **Video RAM:** the types of RAM now mostly used include SGRAM, SDRAM and DDR SDRAM. SGRAM is currently the state-of-the-art graphics memory option. It can run at speeds of 133MHz or more and work easily with the new breed of motherboards capable of 133MHz+ bus speeds. SGRAM is ideally suited to PCI- and AGP-based video cards.

  A typical video card memory (RAM) today is around 16Mb. Adding more memory can provide a wider range of colours and resolutions and may increase overall video speed. So video memory of 32Mb-64Mb using fast SDRAM, double speed DDR SDRAM or even faster DDR SGRAM is the ideal choice to help ensure fast 2D/3D graphics and improved games performance.

- **Video BIOS:** contains the simple routines that link the video card electronic chips to the software on your PC.

- **Video chipset:** the chipset and the amount of memory determine the video card speed and range of resolutions available. Most graphics cards today use either one of two popular chipsets:

- **nVIDIA:** this chipset now dominates the graphics chipset market. The very fast nVIDIA TNT2 chipset is often used in budget graphics cards.

- **GeForce 256:** typical memory of 16Mb. Also, 4Mb, 8Mb and 32Mb varieties are available.

The VGA specification

Since the PC was invented by IBM in 1981, several different graphics standards have emerged and subsequently been superseded by ever faster display technologies. Today, the Video Graphics Array (VGA) standard is the dominant benchmark.

A video card for a current PC needs to match the VGA standard. An enhancement is the Super VGA (SVGA) card which can display at resolutions of 800 x 600 or higher.

Most SVGA video cards also use a standard 15-pin video connector to connect to the display monitor, so that any new monitor using this connector should function with any SVGA video card.

The video driver

A video driver is the customised software that enables your PC's operating system to work with your particular type of video card. Key point: having the correct video driver is essential for best results.

When choosing a video card, it's important to ensure your card includes the necessary software drivers, and that you can easily switch between the different resolutions available to you. Microsoft Windows includes a wide range of video drivers for different video cards. These can usually be manually installed (if necessary) using the Windows Control Panel.

Video card specifications include the refresh rate, which represents how steady an image appears on the screen. Refresh rate is measured in Hertz (Hz) and should be at least 72Hz at the resolution you're viewing (e.g. 800 x 600 pixels). The higher the refresh rate, the less screen flicker you'll experience.

Choosing a video card

The faster a video card runs, the faster the images display. In the continuing quest for faster response, one of the latest components is the Accelerated Graphics Port (AGP). If your motherboard has an AGP slot, then usually a fast AGP video card that is compatible with your motherboard is your preferred option. If your motherboard does not have an AGP slot, you can use a PCI video card instead.

Some motherboards come with video circuitry already built in. However, these rarely provide the power and range of features often found on separate video cards. With these motherboards, you may still be able to use an external video card if you can disable the relevant video circuitry on the motherboard first.

The GrafixStar 750 from Videologic

Currently, AGP 4x is the fastest AGP standard available. If your motherboard has an AGP slot, and you want a faster AGP video card, check whether your motherboard can accept the AGP 4x video card you want. AGP 1x is now obsolete while AGP 2x is now considered a slow/ minimum specification.

Also, consider the amount of video RAM you'll need. In Microsoft Windows, 2Mb of video RAM is the accepted minimum standard and can provide 1,600 x 1,200 resolution in 256 colours. Most cards currently come with 8Mb+.

If you're performing serious DTP, graphic design, video or photographic manipulation work, then you'll probably want at least 16Mb-32Mb of video memory providing 16.7 million colours at 1,280 x 1,024 resolution or higher. Some high-performance cards are also available with 64Mb.

An average video card provides a resolution of up to 1,024 x 768 using up to 16 million colours with a minimum refresh rate of 75Hz. Many of today's 'standard' video cards can also handle multimedia files and 3D panoramas superbly.

Video cards for high-end applications may use the Double Data Rate Synchronous Graphics memory (DDR SGRAM). However, this is still quite expensive for all but the most demanding of applications. If a video card has a 'features' connector, you may be able to combine other functions by fitting TV tuners, video capture boards and video playback (MPEG) boards.

Multimedia cards

Standard video cards are essential for displaying text and images produced on a PC. However, if you want to work with video clips, 3D animation, and other quick-change video sequences, you'll probably need an especially powerful and fast video adaptor with a chipset designed to support the current popular video standards, like MPEG (Motion Pictures Expert Group).

If you want to view video clips from other sources like Indio, Cinipack and other AVI clips, make sure your intended video adaptor supports the standards you need.

MPEG is a standard used to convert TV and film files into a format that a PC can read and display.

If you want to work with video files, you'll need lots of hard disk space. Although video files are heavily compressed, they can still take up a surprising amount of hard drive space. Aim for a minimum hard drive capacity of 5Gb, and ideally, choose a new, fast video card that includes the new VESA Video Interface Port (VESA VIP).

The VESA Video Interface Port (Vesa VIP)

The VESA VIP is designed especially to handle several video streams simultaneously and to connect with third-party multimedia devices like MPEG devices, decoders, digitizers, encoders, and so on. VESA VIP is available in several versions; key point: make sure that both the VESA VIP card you want and the third-party device to which it connects are mutually compatible.

3D graphics accelerators

3D computerised images, although not true 3D (a display monitor is a 2D technology), can provide an amazing amount of detail. To make this detail clearly visible, sometimes a special type of graphics card is needed, one that includes a chipset designed to handle 3D. If 3D is for you, discuss what's on offer with your supplier.

Installing a video card

New video cards are Plug-and-Play-compatible, which essentially allows Microsoft Windows to automatically recognise and configure a Plug-and-Play video card.

However, problems can still arise if you're working with an older video card or motherboard when either or both are not Plug-and-Play-compatible. In this case, you'll probably have to install the video drivers manually using the Windows Control Panel.

Currently, the fastest video cards are those designed for a motherboard containing an Accelerated Graphics Port (AGP) slot. Otherwise, a PCI-based video card is the next best option. The older, slower ISA slot video cards are now essentially obsolete.

If your chosen video card and PC are both truly Plug-and-Play compatible, then the job of installing and setting up is already made much easier for you.

Before unpacking your card from its antistatic bag, remember to observe the antistatic precautions listed in Chapter One, page 14. Carefully read the documentation that comes with your card and perform the exact installation instructions. However, as a general guide, consider the following guidelines for installing a new video card.

If you plan to add more RAM to your video card, make sure the extra video RAM you obtain is designed specifically for your video card, or fully compatible with it. If you install electronic chips, usually, you can identify pin 1 by looking for a marker like a dot or small square.

1 Ensure your PC is switched off and the mains lead is disconnected from the system. Make sure you have the antistatic wrist strap attached to equalise any static electricity in your body throughout the PC.

2 Remove the PC's case and unscrew the retaining screw securing the old video card. Carefully unplug any leads connected to the old video card and then remove the card from its slot. Store it safely, component side down.

3 Unpack the new video card and install in an appropriate slot. If the card is a PCI device, install in a PCI slot. If the card is an AGP device, install in the AGP slot. Install the new card by holding both ends of the card as shown in the following illustration. While installing, if necessary, carefully rock the card from end to end to push it fully home into the slot.

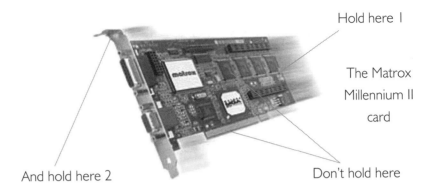

Hold here 1

The Matrox
Millennium II
card

And hold here 2

Don't hold here

If your card already has 8Mb, you may want to add another 8Mb for better performance with 3D applications. Most recent video cards often allow more RAM to be fitted to the card. Often, additional RAM comes in a special module or 'daughter' board form that you plug into a special socket on the video card. Discuss RAM upgrade options with your supplier before buying.

4 Refit the securing screw into the metal mounting plate of the card. Don't overtighten the screw.

5 You can store the old video card in the antistatic bag which contained the new video card.

6 Refit the PC case, video card connecting lead and any other connectors. Switch the PC on and carry out the necessary setup procedures in the software. However, note that Windows may recognise the new card and prompt you to insert the disk or CD-ROM containing the new video driver. The software installation is outlined overleaf.

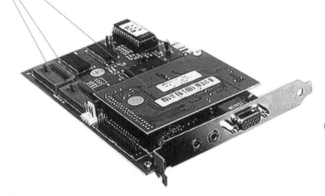

The GrafixStar
400 card with
daughter board
(MPEG) attached

Setting up a video card

After physically installing a new video card, the appropriate video driver software must also be installed. To install the driver for a new video card in Windows, first read the installation documentation that comes with your card. However, the driver installation for recent video cards usually follows a pattern similar to that outlined below.

1   Switch on the PC. Windows will probably detect the new card and prompt you to install the new driver. If a diskette containing the new video driver is provided with the card, make sure the option 'Driver From Disk Provided By Hardware Manufacturer' is chosen, then click OK.

2   In the Install From Disk window, place the diskette containing the new driver into the drive and click OK.

3   When driver installation is complete, if Windows prompts you to restart the PC, remove the diskette, then click Yes.

4   (Optional) Install any other desired software utilities that may be included with your new video card.

If Windows doesn't automatically recognise the new video card when you switch on, you can still install the driver easily using the Add New Hardware Wizard in the Control Panel. Read your Windows documentation for details.

Testing a video card

After installing and setting up your video card as outlined here, if your Microsoft Windows appears normally, your video card is obviously performing its role. However, you may need to make some adjustments on the monitor to reposition the picture on the screen. Alternatively, you may want to adjust the resolution or other settings. The precise procedure for these tasks should be included in your video card or Windows documentation, either printed or through online Help.

Display monitors

A display monitor is arguably one of the most crucial parts of your PC. It's surprising how many people overlook this aspect when buying an entire system. In this chapter, we take a closer look at monitors, their merits and drawbacks.

Covers

Chapter Eleven

Choosing a display monitor

Your monitor is the most obvious link between you and your PC, and as such deserves special consideration. Hint: before purchasing a monitor, view several in action if possible. We all see differently and as 60% of people in the developed world wear glasses or contact lenses, the clarity and crispness of the text and images on a monitor are especially essential if you intend to spend long periods using your PC.

A flicker-free display

Organic Light-Emitting Diodes (OLEDs) were developed some years ago by Kodak, and are now being rediscovered. OLED technology may help create better, brighter, cheaper low power displays. The drawback is these displays may not be available for another year or more.

To ensure a crisp, clear, flicker-free display, consider a monitor with the following minimum specification:

- Screen refresh rate of at least 72Hz at the resolution you intend to work at – usually at least 800 x 600 pixels.

- Capable of non-interlaced display.

- Ideally, a dot pitch of 0.24mm. The smaller the dot pitch, the sharper the image. Other typical dot pitches include: 0.25mm, 0.26mm or 0.28mm.

Key point: the newer flat-panel LCD-type monitors take up less desk space and save electrical power.

Establishing the right size

Ensure your desired monitor will fit on your desk adequately and that the desk is strong enough to support it – especially important if you're planning to buy a 17", or larger, monitor.

If you plan to spend a lot of time in front of a computer monitor, it pays to consider your options carefully. Screen size is calculated by measuring diagonally from the top left corner of the screen to bottom right. However, remember that screen size is not the same as the visible area: the monitor casing and facia covers some of the screen. For example, a 17" screen provides a 15.5" viewing area.

When working with graphically-rich programs like Microsoft Windows, the author considers a 17" screen size to be a minimum requirement when viewing at 800 x 600 resolution – and currently, 17" offers the best value for money!

If you're working with DTP or CAD regularly, 19" is probably the minimum screen size you should consider if your budget will allow – your eyes will thank you for it.

The Iiyama VisionMaster 450 large screen monitor

When cleaning your display monitor screen, use only a small amount of spray on the duster. Make sure you polish off every trace to avoid leaving a film that can cause streaks and irritating reflections that can cause additional eye strain.

Monitors that include Dynamic Power Management Architecture (DPMA) use smart routines to manage power consumption at the chipset level, automatically controlling power and switching to stand-by as needed.

Power considerations

If you want to save power, choose a monitor that conforms to the latest energy-saving criteria. Most monitors available now are Energy Star-compliant (logo shown above). Energy Star is a US standard originally and refers only to electrical consumption. The Standard ensures that a monitor will power down to 30 watts or less in 'Sleep' mode. However, most modern PCs go much further than this: some will power down to less than 5 watts in Sleep mode.

Radiation considerations

It's important to note that the Energy Star development mentioned in the previous paragraph doesn't cover low radiation standards. All display monitors emit some radiation. Obviously, the lower this figure, the better.

Many manufacturers now meet the Swedish MPR II guidelines for reduced electrical and magnetic emissions and certainly this is a good standard at which to aim.

Another safety standard to look for is the TCO-xx recommendations on emissions. TCO-92-compliant sets have to carry the TCO-92 logo shown above. More recent devices should display the TCO-95 or TCO-99 logos.

Updating display monitor software

If you change your monitor, you can easily update Windows to take advantage of any special features your monitor may have – like Energy Star power saving. After switching off your PC, connect the new monitor to the PC and switch on. Carry out the following steps to tell Windows about your new monitor.

1 Click the right mouse button on an empty part of the Windows desktop to display the pop-up context menu.

Depending on which version of Microsoft Windows and monitor type you're using, if you change your monitor, Windows may automatically detect the change and install the required drivers for you.

Most current motherboards support Advanced Power Management (APM). This is a joint Intel–Microsoft initiative providing four power states: On, Stand-by, Suspend and Off, designed to help save power when the monitor is not in use.

2 Click the Properties command.

3 In the Display Properties dialog box, click the Settings tab, then the Advanced button.

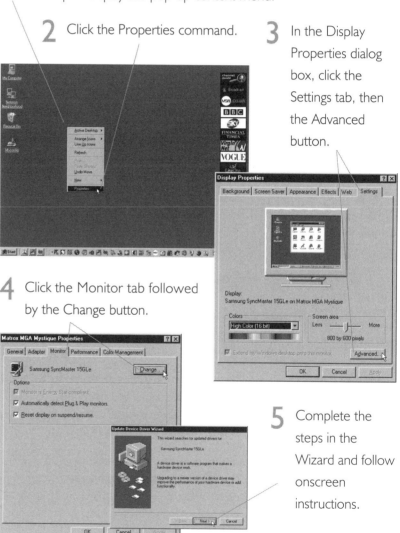

4 Click the Monitor tab followed by the Change button.

5 Complete the steps in the Wizard and follow onscreen instructions.

CD-ROM drives

CD-ROMs are now the preferred delivery medium of most software manufacturers. Moreover, when a CD-ROM drive is coupled to a suitable sound system, it can deliver superb sound quality and video sequences – multimedia. In this chapter, we examine the implications involved in choosing, installing and setting up a CD-ROM drive in a PC.

Covers

Chapter Twelve

CD-ROMs and multimedia

CD-ROM – Compact Disc-Read Only Memory – enables large amounts of information to be stored for quick and easy retrieval later. Multimedia is the combined use of text, sound, still pictures and moving pictures within an application in a PC. CD-ROMs

and multimedia of course are closely related. CD-ROM technology is one of the main ways to see multimedia in action, although DVD-ROMs are expected to become the dominant standard soon.

CD-ROM-based technology is also used in the more recent DVD drives. DVD drives are covered in Chapter Thirteen. Eventually, DVD may replace the CD-ROM to become the favourite software delivery medium.

The CD-ROM standard has resulted in several variations, including: the 'Red Book' standard for audio CDs and 'Yellow Book' to cover PC CD-ROMs. Although a CD-ROM can now store about 650Mb (maximum 682Mb) of data, drive speed is much slower compared to a typical hard drive. Nevertheless, a CD-ROM drive contains some amazingly sophisticated error-checking circuitry to control speed and keep the read head directly over the track currently being read. Most earlier-generation CD-ROM drives used the Constant Linear Velocity (CLV) technique to do this. CLV ensures disk velocity is reduced proportionally as the read head moves from the centre outwards.

Most new multi-speed drives now employ CAV control to provide improved performance. CAV – or Constant Angular Velocity – ensures the disk spins at a constant velocity irrespective of the read head's position. More recently, TrueX or Multibeam technology has also emerged using seven laser beams to help control tracking and

speed up the read (transfer) rate, while reducing noise and vibration.

Using CD-ROMs

In one sense, CD-ROM discs don't wear out: they're only ever read by a scanning laser light so no wear and tear at that point is involved. However, once removed from the CD-ROM drive, they're vulnerable to scratches/physical damage.

Not all CD-ROMs are made the same; with pirate copying unfortunately becoming more common, substandard CD-ROMs may be available. Best advice: steer well clear of these cheap pirated copies; not only are they illegal but they may damage your drive.

If you remove the outer cover of a CD-ROM drive, make sure the PC/CD-ROM drive is powered off: even the low power laser light from a CD-ROM drive's laser can damage the human eye. Be careful.

Older CD-ROM drives may have problems trying to read the latest CD-ROMs. Why: newer CD-ROMs can store more data – over 650Mb. Earlier disks could only store about 550Mb.

Best advice: use only those CD-ROMs which meet the 'Red Book' and 'Yellow Book' standards, bearing the genuine CD-ROM logos.

Cleaning CD-ROM drive optical lenses

Many CD-ROM drives available now include a built-in lens cleaning system. Over time, the CD-ROM lens may develop a layer of dirt causing mis-focusing and mis-tracking. Although you may be able to remove the drive, dismantle it and gently clean the lens with isopropyl alcohol and a cotton bud, if you choose to do this, take extreme care: too much pressure and the lens assembly may break.

Best solution: buy a CD-ROM lens cleaning kit and follow its guidelines.

Handling CD-ROMs

A common error is to think optical media like CD-ROMs and DVDs are indestructible. Not true. Although small scratches and some fingerprint marks should not affect a disk, deep scratches may cause mis-tracking and other errors. To maintain your CD-ROMs and keep them in top condition, consider the following guidelines:

To reduce the chances of scratching a CD/DVD, try to avoid stacking individual discs on top of one another. Ideally, store vertically – like books in a bookcase – and keep in a protective sleeve when not in use.

CD-ROM and DVD disk drive trays are easily broken when left in the open position. Best advice: develop the habit of always closing the drive tray as soon as possible.

- Pick up CD-ROMs by holding the outer edges and centre hole; avoid touching the disk surface. Why? You avoid the risk of transferring a thin film of grease onto the disk.

- Don't clean a CD-ROM unless you really have to. Then, use a soft, dry cloth and gently wipe in short strokes from the inside edge directly towards the outer rim (radially), working around the disk.

- Always store the disks in their sleeves or cases when not in use to reduce the possibility of damage from objects being placed upon them.

- Avoid writing on a disk. As a last resort, you can write on the label side using a special soft marker pen available from computer dealers. Don't use a ballpoint pen or pencil: the nibs are too hard.

- Don't bend CD-ROMs.

- Keep all CD-ROMs away from strong sunlight, high temperature or environments with a high humidity.

- When you've finished using a CD-ROM disk, it's not a bad idea to develop the habit of putting it back into its protective case, to reduce the likelihood of any possible damage.

Choosing a CD-ROM drive

Current CD-ROM drives are now mostly 50x speed – or faster. The higher the speed, the higher the data transfer rate. Although, usually, more speed means more vibration too, the 100x speed technology from the Elite Group works by copying the CD-ROM contents to the hard drive and then accessing the cached copy rather than the CD-ROM directly.

Most important buying considerations

Consider the following guidelines:

If you want to use rewriteable CD-ROMs (CD-RW) as well as play CD-ROMs, ideally, purchase both a CD-ROM (player) drive and a separate CD-RW drive. Why: usually, CD-RW drives run much slower than CD-ROM drives. If you spend more time playing CDs than recording, you'll free up some time.

- Speed: you want a drive as fast as possible. A fast speed is particularly important when playing back CDs containing any fast moving video-type sequences. Slower speeds may produce fragmented playback quality. Ideally opt for at least a 52x speed drive.

- Data transfer rate: (can also be improved by using a faster CPU) a 52x speed drive should transfer about 7.5Kb of data each second.

- Access time: the lower the drive's average access time, the better – try to aim for 80ms or less.

- Connection method: how do you want to connect your drive: IDE, SCSI, parallel port or USB? See overleaf.

- Disk loading system: most use a drive tray. More rarely, you may still be able to buy a drive that uses a caddy instead, or a feeding slot.

- Horizontal/vertical drive: can the drive be installed vertically as well as horizontally? Is this feature important?

- Built-in lens cleaning: many drives now include built-in lens cleaning: a valuable feature.

- Noise and vibration levels: are they tolerable for you?

- Tray build quality: is the tray held firmly in the guide rails? Is the tray action smooth?

- Software drivers: does your operating system support the drive you want to use?

E-IDE, SCSI, parallel, or USB-based CD-ROM drives

The type of interface used to connect a CD-ROM drive to a PC usually determines its performance and cost, amongst other factors. IDE CD-ROM drives, like their hard drive cousins, can offer good performance for low cost.

Usually, SCSI CD-ROM drives are faster than their IDE equivalents but may cost more. Drives that connect to a PC's parallel (printer) port are usually much slower, whereas the latest USB v2.0-compatible drives offer a much faster solution.

If your PC has the fast USB version 2.0-compatible connectors and you're using Windows 98, Me, XP or 2000, a USB-based CD-RW drive combined with the now low cost of CD-RW disks can provide an excellent backup solution. See Chapter Seven for more information.

If you need high power and fast response, with price considerations coming second, then SCSI or USB may be ideal for you. SCSI drives are usually more expensive and require the additional purchase of a special host adapter card if one is not already present in your PC.

Nevertheless, CD-ROM manufacturers are now producing some very fast E-IDE drives and some have been shown to equal SCSI models in recent reputable speed tests.

A features check list

Many good CD-ROM drives include the following:

*   Play/skip button

*   Headphones socket

*   Volume control

*   Disk activity light

*   Dust protection feature: this may be a simple seal around the perimeter of the drive tray

*   An easy-to-understand user guide, including instructions for installing in different operating systems

*   Meets the Multimedia PC (MPC) Level-2/Level-3 standards

Installing a CD-ROM drive

Installing a USB-based CD-ROM drive

The Universal Serial Bus (USB) offers a usually simple solution to adding a CD-ROM drive to a PC. The USB standard is available in v1.1 and the much faster v2.0. Follow the simple installation instructions, connect your USB lead both ends and follow the onscreen instructions to let Microsoft Windows install the necessary drivers.

Installing an internal drive to an IDE interface

Originally, only two hard drives could be attached to an IDE interface, one master and one slave on a single channel. The more recent E-IDE specification includes a second channel, allowing connection of up to four devices, including a CD-ROM drive.

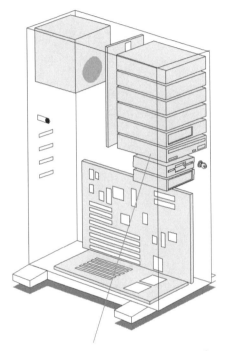

If possible, though, don't install a CD-ROM drive on the same channel as a hard drive. Why? The hard drive controller circuits will almost certainly slow down the speed of the hard drive to match

Full tower PCs have plenty of room to add peripherals like CD-ROM drives

that of the CD-ROM drive. Remember, hard drives usually run at a much faster rate than CD-ROM drives, so we don't want to do anything that might risk slowing the speed of the hard drive or affecting its data transfer rate.

If your PC has two IDE-type hard drives, if possible, install the CD-ROM drive to the secondary IDE channel with the hard drives installed as master and slave on the primary channel. This can ensure the slower CD-ROM device does not affect the usually faster hard drives.

Installing an IDE-based CD-ROM drive

First switch off the PC and disconnect the power lead. Next, attach your antistatic wrist strap. Read your installation guide and perform the installation steps. Then, remove the PC casing. For general reference, consider the guidelines below.

1 Set the configuration jumper on the CD-ROM drive to the correct position: usually master, slave or cable select.

2 Establish the empty drive bay where you want to install your drive and carefully install the drive using the supplied screws.

3 Attach the appropriate 40-pin IDE connector, remembering to align pin 1 on the lead with pin 1 on the socket. Usually, pin 1 on the lead has a coloured strip on the ribbon cable.

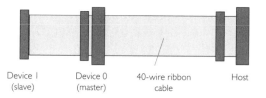

Device 1   Device 0   40-wire ribbon   Host
(slave)   (master)   cable

4 Attach the power connector to the drive. The connector should fit in easily only one way.

5 Install the appropriate software driver as outlined on the next page.

Setting up a CD-ROM drive

If you use Windows 95/98/Me/XP/NT/2000

CD-ROM drives purchased from reputable suppliers should meet the Attachment Packet Interface (ATAPI) IDE standard. Installing an ATAPI IDE drive in Windows 95/98/Me/XP/NT/2000 should then be a simple process: Windows should contain all the software drivers you need. Just follow the steps below.

1 After physically installing the CD-ROM drive, when you power up the PC, Windows automatically checks your PC hardware for any changes.

If your version of Microsoft Windows does not automatically install the software drivers for your CD-ROM drive, you can manually start the Add New Hardware Wizard from its icon in the Windows Control Panel and complete the necessary steps yourself.

2 When Windows detects the new CD-ROM drive, it automatically installs the appropriate driver. Windows may display the Add New Hardware Wizard, as shown below. Follow the onscreen instructions.

3 More rarely, Windows may ask for the floppy disk containing the latest software driver. Your CD-ROM may come supplied with this driver if necessary.

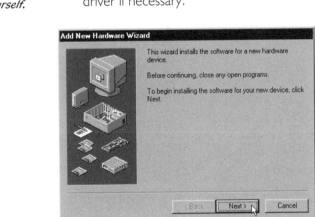

4 When you reboot, Windows should identify the new CD-ROM drive.

Older PCs, operating systems and CD-ROM drives

If your PC is not Plug-and-Play compliant, or you're using a Microsoft Windows operating system before Windows 95, then setup can be quite tricky.

You'll need access to all the relevant older documentation and you may need additional drivers – which may not even be available any more. These older systems can become dated quickly. Therefore, the simple solution is to avoid this if at all possible and consider other upgrade options.

If you have a considerably older PC (five years+), often the only realistic economical upgrade option would be to simply buy a new or more up-to-date PC, rather than try to patch up the old one.

Testing your installation

Often a CD-ROM drive is included as part of a multimedia installation: that is, including a sound card and speakers. You can easily check the installation by simply placing an audio CD in the CD-ROM drive.

Microsoft Windows then usually activates the AutoPlay function and the CD should start playing. When the CD is playing, click on the CD Player button on the Windows Task bar to display the CD Player window, as  shown here, from where you can stop and start, jump forward or backward and so on. Note: your particular version of Windows determines the look and feel of your installed Player, so may be different from our illustration above.

DVD drives

A Digital Versatile Disc (DVD) drive offers some amazing and exciting possibilities for a PC and indeed other home- and business-based entertainment systems. Here, we examine what DVD-ROM actually is; how to choose the right DVD drive for your PC system and how to install it successfully first time.

Covers

Chapter Thirteen

DVD basics

The DVD-ROM (Digital Versatile Disc) – which essentially is a supercharged CD-ROM – is emerging not only as the obvious replacement for video tapes, but also as an ideal medium for connection to a range of audio- and video-based multimedia devices.

 A standard CD-ROM today can store up to about 680Mb of digital information. A 'standard' DVD disc however, can store about 7 times that capacity (4.7Gb).

 Two types of DVDs are available. DVD-ROM discs contain computer data and software, whereas DVD-Video discs are designed for DVD-Video players and TV/sound systems.

DVD-ROM discs are available in single-sided or double-sided varieties and each side can have a single layer or double layer. So what is so special about DVD-ROM? Here's why DVD-ROM technology is causing so much excitement:

• Current DVD-ROMs can store up to 4.7Gb of digital information on a single-sided, single-layer disc using material that is the same size and thickness as a standard CD-ROM disc today.

• A single-sided dual layer disc can now store up to 8.5Gb while a two-sided single layer disc can reach about 9.4Gb.

• Two-sided discs containing two layers can currently store up to an amazing 17Gb of information!

• Compared to a CD-ROM drive, a DVD-ROM drive runs very fast, allowing greater capacity and faster response.

• One of the most exciting features is that a DVD drive can also play today's standard PC CD-ROMs as well as audio CDs.

• An amazing range of prerecorded movies are now available in DVD format, with more being added daily.

• Each current DVD can hold approximately 135 minutes of high quality video and CD-quality sound. This can be increased to 160 minutes by using a single audio track (mono).

- DVD-ROM drives usually use the standard PC interface connectors: IDE and SCSI, making the job of installation much easier.

A DVD-ROM disc spins at about three times the speed of the original single-speed CD-ROM. The 4x- and 16x-speed drives are now well established. Currently, the fastest 16x-speed drives are equivalent to an amazing 144x-speed CD-ROM drive and provide a data transfer rate of over 22Mb (22 million bytes) each second!

Some of the more recent DVD-ROM drives can also play back CD-R and CD-RW CD-ROMs in addition to standard CDs.

Recordable DVD-ROM drives

One major drawback with the type of DVD-ROM drive examined so far is that you cannot erase the content and re-record new content. So currently, these 'standard' DVD-ROM drives are really only extremely powerful playback devices.

With some DVD-ROM drives, you may also need to purchase a separate MPEG-2 sound card. Some drives include a MPEG-2 card as part of a 'kit' whereas other, more recent drive makers build the MPEG circuitry directly into the DVD drive electronics.

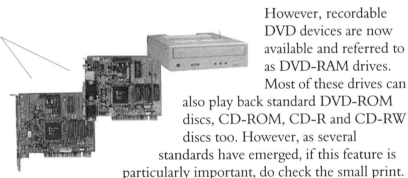

However, recordable DVD devices are now available and referred to as DVD-RAM drives. Most of these drives can also play back standard DVD-ROM discs, CD-ROM, CD-R and CD-RW discs too. However, as several standards have emerged, if this feature is particularly important, do check the small print.
DVD-RAM drives are rapidly becoming mainstream products as prices fall to realistic levels.

Firewire (IEEE 1394): a fast bus standard

Firewire – a recently developed, fast, computer communications technology – has been developed to cater especially for the high demands of today's multimedia devices, like DVD-ROM and DVD-RAM drives.

This standard allows for data to be transferred at an amazing 400Mbps and is already supported in Windows 98, Me, XP, NT and 2000. Firewire is now also being used more often for hard drives, tape drives, CD-ROM and other optical drives, and so on.

Choosing a DVD drive

DVD-ROM drives, like CD-ROM and hard drives usually come in two main types: IDE and SCSI (see Chapter Five for more information outlining the differences).

Buying a DVD-ROM drive

You can buy some DVD-ROM drives as an 'upgrade kit'. Often, these kits can include a special video quality booster in the form of an MPEG add-on board, that usually installs into an available PCI slot on your motherboard. Sometimes however, some smaller MPEG boards can attach to suitable existing sound boards as a 'daughter board'.

The MPEG board ensures that the DVD-ROM player can properly display and play fast-moving video components stored on a DVD-ROM disc.

Some of the latest DVD-ROM players go one stage further and simply integrate the MPEG board directly into the DVD-ROM player structure, making the job of installation and setup even easier. You can easily identify these types of 'integrated' DVD-ROM drive by the 'DVD MPEG-2 accelerated' description often used in the accompanying sales material.

Remember also, you can now buy a DVD-ROM drive for playback only, or for recording and playing back your own material (see previous page).

Installing your DVD drive

Installing a DVD-ROM drive into a fully compliant Windows Plug-and-Play (PnP) system is usually straightforward, as Windows 95/98/Me/XP/NT/2000 contains all the software drivers you need to ensure the DVD-ROM drive works correctly. Remember, a 'driver' is simply the special software that makes the device work directly with your computer's operating system.

To install your DVD-ROM drive, first read the maker's instructions carefully. Remember, you'll either use an IDE interface connector or a SCSI interface connector. You need to know which one you're using and the appropriate interface must already be installed, available and set up properly. First perform steps 1 to 3 below:

Try to avoid connecting a DVD-ROM drive and main hard drive on the same channel, to prevent the response of both devices being slowed down.

Most modern motherboards have an IDE adaptor/ interface built into the motherboard. To easily identify a built-in IDE/ adaptor, look for the connectors labelled 'IDE Primary channel' and 'IDE Secondary channel'.

1 Switch off your PC and remove the power lead from the mains socket.

2 After fitting your antistatic wrist strap as outlined on page 14, remove the outer casing to your PC.

3 Establish whether you are using an IDE connection of a SCSI connection, then set up the relevant connector or interface as discussed below and overleaf.

IDE DVD preparation: pre-installation setup

Remember, a modern PC usually has at least two IDE channels and each channel can support up to two devices. So for example, you might have your main hard drive plugged into the primary IDE channel and set up as a master and your (slower) CD-ROM drive on the same channel set up therefore as a slave device.

In this example, ideally a better option might be to first consider installing and setting up your DVD-ROM drive as a master device on the secondary channel. Then move and reconnect your CD-ROM drive as a slave device on the DVD-ROM channel. Usually, you can alter a jumper on the drive to establish your desired master or slave setting.

SCSI DVD drive pre-installation configuration

Setting up a SCSI adapter can often be easier than installing a device under IDE. All you need do is install a SCSI card as covered on pages 52-53 and apply the instructions that come with your SCSI card. If you already have a SCSI card installed properly, you only need choose an appropriate SCSI ID number (not 0 or 7 though as these are usually reserved for the SCSI card and the SCSI system).

Finally, if your DVD-ROM drive is the last device in your SCSI chain, remember to terminate it properly as outlined on page 53 and in your DVD-ROM documentation. Next:

4 Now configure your DVD-ROM drive as a master or a slave, whichever is appropriate for the status you have decided on.

If your PC has only one hard drive connected to the Primary channel, if possible, install your almost certainly slower DVD-ROM drive to the secondary channel to avoid slowing the hard drive.

5 Install the DVD-ROM drive into your PC following the maker's instructions. Secure using appropriate screws.

6 Attach the DVD-ROM data interface connector cable, making sure that it is correctly aligned (pin 1 to socket 1).

7 Attach the power cable securely.

8 Reconnect the PC power lead and switch on. If you're using Windows 95/98/Me/XP/NT/2000, Windows may automatically install the relevant software drivers for you. Otherwise, see the maker's instructions for installing manually.

9 Reboot your PC. You can quickly confirm that your new DVD-ROM drive has been recognised by Windows by first moving to or starting up Windows Explorer. Then scroll down until you see the new drive icon representing your DVD-ROM drive.

Test your drive installation by inserting and playing a DVD-ROM disc and optionally performing a test recording.

Audio processing devices

A sound card can provide high-quality audio functions to a PC, and is also a primary component in any multimedia installation. In this chapter, we examine the business of purchasing, installing and setting up a sound card and using a microphone or headset.

Covers

Chapter Fourteen

An overview of PC sound files

PCs use two main types of sound files:

- **Recorded source:** these are made up from sounds recorded outside of the PC and include file formats with the filename extensions of .wav, .aiff, .au, and .voc.

- **MIDI:** Musical Instrument Digital Interface (MIDI) is a standard designed to allow musical instruments and a PC to share data. MIDI files, identified by the .mid filename extension, are purely digital in content and contain special code that instructs the hardware exactly how to create the desired sound. MIDI files can also be easily edited on a PC.

Most MP3 music files are protected by copyright. Downloading and distributing files or information that are already protected by copyright without the agreed payment is illegal, and may result in prosecution.

Check out www.mp3.com/ for more information about what's available in MP3 format.

More about MIDI sound files

Professional musicians often use MIDI to compose and create their musical masterpieces. MIDI can create sounds in two ways: FM synthesis or Wavetable synthesis.

FM synthesis can produce sounds that basically mimic musical instruments and human speech, although the results are not usually realistic.

Wavetable synthesis, however, produces much better, higher quality and more realistic results, using genuine recordings of the human voice and musical instruments. Wavetable synthesis is only usually available on the more expensive sound cards.

Introducing MP3

MP3 is a CD quality, highly compressed sound format that has become popular on the web. Provided you already have a sound card installed, with speakers or headphones, using an MP3 'ripper' utility like Winamp, you can convert any existing sound file or CD music into MP3 format. However, remember to observe any copyright laws that might apply to what you want to copy (see margin).

If you want to compress MP3 files to upload to a website, you can also use tools like RealProducer G2 to prepare the sound files. For more information, visit: www.real.com/

Choosing a sound card

Sound cards are most often used simply for playing multimedia applications, presentations, and audio CDs. With suitable speakers and/or headphones, you can also enjoy stereo sound reproduction.

Buying decisions

Most important advice: ensure your proposed sound card is Sound Blaster-compatible and is available in PCI format. This usually ensures maximum compatibility with

Sound Blaster PCI128

Many sound card makers provide a power level of about 4–6 watts per channel, but some are certainly more powerful. Make sure your speakers can handle the power output of the sound card without damage.

most PCs. However, as always, check with your supplier that your proposed sound card is fully compatible with your system. Not all so-called 'Sound Blaster-compatible' boards are *truly* compatible with the Sound Blaster standard, so beware.

If you want top-quality sound, a sound card from the Sound Blaster 64 series or equivalent is an ideal choice if your budget will allow. Buying a sound card can involve considering a range of factors. The following list includes some additional points to consider:

- If you play Microsoft Windows games, choose a sound card that is compatible with DirectX and A3D.

- Ensure your sound card is Plug-and-Play compatible.

- How many 'voices' can it reproduce? In music files, the number of voices relates to the number of instruments which can be played; 32 voices is good, 64 is much better.

- Does it include data compression for recording and playback of music and speech?

- Your sound card should easily meet the Multimedia PC MPC Level-3 specification. Forget Level-2 – it's out of date.

- Does it have stereo or quadraphonic sound reproduction capability?

- Sampling rate: usually 16-bit or 32-bit.

- Sound samples stored in a ROM chip: your card may include 1–3 Mb of samples.

- For games users, does it have a game port (joystick socket)?

- Or a sound mixer facility?

- Facility to connect add-on wavetable sub-boards for even better sound quality.

- Line in and line out jack sockets; microphone and speaker out sockets.

- MIDI synthesizer interface and connector if you're keen on high-quality music and want to connect a music keyboard to your PC.

- Is 3D sound supported?

- Does the range of any bundled software meet your needs?

- Some sound cards include a volume control, although this facility is not usually necessary as the control software should include a range of sound controls and options.

Choosing speakers

Speakers are the last link in the sound chain. However good your sound card may be, it's wasted if the speakers are of poor quality. If possible, visit a showroom and listen to a range of speakers before deciding on a final choice: your ears will tell you what is right for you.

Check that the speaker leads are long enough for your particular system: some makers may skimp here. *Most importantly, make sure the speakers you choose can handle the power output of the amplifier, otherwise inadequate speakers and the sound card may be damaged.*

Consider the following buying guidelines:

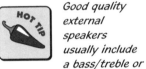

Good quality external speakers usually include a bass/treble or tone control, volume knob and on-off switch also.

- **Power output per channel:** measured in watts RMS. Usually in the range of 10–30 watts per channel.

- **Frequency response:** a high-quality card will reproduce the low-frequency sounds at 20Hz through to the high-frequency sounds at 20,000Hz.

- **Distortion:** measured in per cent (%). The lower the percentage figure, the better.

Dynamic Bass Boost (DBB)

A Dynamic Bass Boost (DBB) switch allows you to enhance the bass and treble sound quality, irrespective of the volume setting you're using. When the volume level changes, our ears can generally become less sensitive to higher frequency notes – a DBB compensates to correct this mismatch.

Powered speakers

These are simply speakers with audio amplifiers built into the speaker boxes, instead of on the sound card. Usually, standard sound cards don't provide much sound power output. To gain a greater level of sound with more control, powered speakers are available. Powered hi-fi speakers are also ideal if you want to provide high-quality sound for a business presentation or a multimedia show.

Installing a sound card

Physically installing a sound card is easy: you follow a similar procedure to that outlined on page 85. *Setting up* a sound card, however, can be amazingly simple or provide one of the most challenging of upgrade tasks.

Why might a sound card cause so much trouble? Answer: currently, most sound cards takes up more resources than any other add-on. Typically, a sound card needs:

- Multiple Input/Output (I/O) addresses

- Often at least 2 DMA channels

- At least 1 IRQ (usually only 16 are available)

Recent PCs and sound cards should be fully Plug-and-Play-compatible. If so, installing in a Microsoft Windows PC is usually straightforward. Consider the following steps.

Whenever you upgrade, before you make any changes, note down your original settings for any card or device you change. Then, if you run into problems, you can at least restore your original settings quickly and easily while investigating further.

Don't be too concerned if jargon terms like I/O, DMA and IRQs don't make much sense to you. Often, you only need to know the basics to install your sound card. Usually more information is available in the documentation that comes with your sound card.

1 Read the documentation that comes with your sound card.

2 Identify your sound card's requirements for settings.

3 If possible, keep the default settings on the sound card.

4 If your sound card conflicts with another device in your system, *consider changing the settings of the other device* rather than those on the sound card.

Choosing an expansion slot

Sometimes, you may not have a choice in deciding where to put your sound card: there may only be one empty slot remaining. In this event, if you run into compatibility problems, it may even be worthwhile removing all nonessential cards, then installing the sound card followed by the other remaining cards. However, this is a last resort as it is a task that may become quite time-consuming.

However, if you do have a choice, it's always a good idea to try and leave some space between adjacent expansion cards, to allow for extra ventilation and to reduce the possibility of any cross interference between the various cards. To install a sound card, follow the instructions which come with your card. As a general guide, consider these steps.

1   Ensure that the connecting cables reach the card and that there are no other factors affecting physical installation.

Usually, the easiest installation is one in which the sound card is installed before any others (except for the video card). If possible try to use the sound card's default settings rather than change them to match any other cards later.

2   Remove the screw holding the metal blanking plate next to the slot you're using.

3   Carefully hold the sound card by the metal mounting bracket and opposite card edge. Don't touch the edge connectors.

4   If your sound card has adjustable jumpers, set them to the correct positions. See your documentation for exact details.

If you're installing a sound card in a PC running Microsoft Windows, depending on your particular sound card and the version of Windows you're using, Windows may itself install all you need without having to use any further disks.

5   If the CD-ROM drive has a 4-pin audio cable, connect one end of this to the sound card, the other to the internal CD-ROM drive. This connector is usually keyed to ensure you install it the correct way; if not, check your documentation.

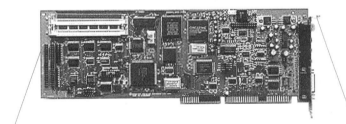

6   Holding the card by its metal mounting bracket and opposite edge, carefully push the card into the expansion slot. Replace the mounting screw to hold the card securely.

7   Plug in your speakers to the appropriate jack socket on the sound card. You're now ready to set up the sound card by installing the driver software. See your Windows guide.

Using a microphone or headset

Most sound boards contain at least:

- A Line-in socket

- A microphone input (Mic-in) socket

- Speaker (out) connection sockets

With the ever increasing use of Internet Chat, and (currently) cheap long distance Internet telephony, you can easily talk to someone, a friend or colleague, on the other side of the globe using a suitable headset, sound board, appropriate software and your dial-up Internet connection.

Microphones

For a microphone to work correctly, it must match the settings of your sound board. Therefore, before buying, examine your sound card documentation and determine the impedance required.

A common PC microphone impedance is 600 ohms. Arguably, a condenser-type microphone can work well with most boards. However, most PC microphones should work; speak to your PC dealer to discuss your specific needs and to obtain a suitable model.

Usually, a microphone attaches to a sound card to a small round jack socket often labelled the 'Mic in' connector. A jack socket contains a single hole in which to place the jack plug.

Once you have a suitable microphone attached and set up, you can record sound/voice files in Windows 95/98/Me/XP/NT/2000. See your Windows documentation for details.

Computer headsets

You can combine speakers and a microphone conveniently in a headset. Then you can set up appropriate software so if you're answering the telephone, you can have both hands free for typing or other Windows-based tasks while talking.

Network cards

A single PC today is an incredibly powerful tool once you're really familiar with how to use it. Two or more PCs linked together forming a network can multiply this effect many times. In this chapter, you can learn about PC networking and how to create a simple network using the built-in networking features of Microsoft Windows.

Covers

Chapter Fifteen

Introduction to PC networking

What is a computer network?

Simply any number of components that enable people to share computer-based information easily. These 'components', in the most basic sense, can be thought of as a collection of interconnected computers, peripherals and related equipment.

Broadly, three main network 'models' are in use today:

At its most basic, the Internet is simply a vast collection of linked computer networks spanning the entire globe: the ultimate network of networks!

- Local Area Network (LAN) refers to those components that are connected at the same location, either physically using wires, or through a wireless solution such as a transmitter/receiver system that uses either infrared (IRDA) or radio waves.

- Wide Area Network (WAN) is the result of linking together various LANs from different locations across a country (or even globally).

An Extranet is a type of Intranet. The main difference: an Extranet shares some content with customers, suppliers and other organizations, but is not open to the general public.

- The Intranet is another hugely popular network model to emerge in recent years, closely related to the Internet (see margin). An Intranet uses the same efficient navigation structure as the Internet but applies it to a private area only – just like a LAN.

Why bother to use a network?

Using a network, people can easily share data files, application software, emails, sound, video and image files, printers, CD-ROM/DVD-ROM drives, faxes and so on.

Without a network, people can waste time getting data into and out of their 'space'. For sharing data among a large number of users, an Intranet is ideal. Whichever type of network is used, it's important to keep information up to date, and sometimes, especially in large, fast-paced organizations, this presents one of the greatest day-to-day challenges.

What do you need to set up a network?

In this chapter, we're going to describe the 'Peer-to-peer' network, as the software for this is built into Microsoft Windows. Therefore, to create a network, in addition to Microsoft Windows 95/98/Me/XP/NT/2000, we use: at least two PCs; the network cabling and infrastructure; a Network Interface Card (NIC) for each PC/workstation; and a compatible network hub (explained in more depth on page 128).

Firewall defined: a software/hardware solution created to protect a network from unauthorised access and to keep data secure.

To set up a 'Fast Ethernet' system, you need to ensure that the network Hub, all cables and all Network Interface Cards, are all designed for 100Mbps operation.

In fibre-optic cable, data travels in the form of light bursts rather than electrical pulses. Main benefit: any light-based system does not suffer from electromagnetic interference.

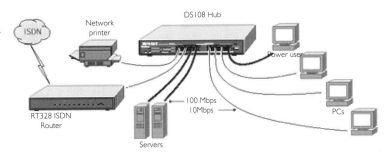

Introduction to Ethernet

Simply put, Ethernet provides a standard way to move data quickly around a computer network. It's one of the easiest, cheapest and most effective ways to establish a network quickly. Ethernet is compatible with many different types of equipment, for example: PCs, Apple Macs, printers, Sun workstations, UNIX workstations and so on. Another reason for Ethernet's success lies in the fast data speeds that are now possible: from the old 10Mbps to the now standard 100Mbps of today's 'Fast Ethernet' networks.

Network cabling and cable connectors

Network cable is available in three broad varieties: (1) Twisted Pair: shielded (STP) and unshielded (UTP), (2) Coaxial (Thin and Thick), and (3) in fibre-optic form (the most expensive). Twisted pair is made shielded – a twisted inner core surrounded by an insulator (shield) – or unshielded (without the insulator). Nowadays, coaxial has been replaced mostly by UTP and is available in two main varieties: 10BaseT (currently the most popular) and 100BaseT.

Types of computer network

In this chapter, we're particularly interested in LAN-based networks. Essentially, three main types are in common use today:

- Client/server.

- Peer-to-peer.

- Hybrid: both Client/server and Peer-to-peer co-existing on the same network (often the most popular choice today for mid- to larger-sized networks).

Client/server

For situations in which data security and control is particularly important, a Peer-to-peer network would probably not represent a good choice. A Client/server LAN can provide much greater security.

A Server is a powerful PC containing the 'central pool' of knowledge or data. Here the Server shares its resources among the Clients. A Client PC usually only communicates with the Server and not directly with other clients on the network (except via the Server).

Often, to provide improved backup security, two Servers on the LAN may run concurrently so that each 'mirrors' the other. Then, if problem occur with one Server, the other takes over and keeps the LAN operational.

Even small organizations with only four or five networked PCs can benefit from a Client/server network, especially if regularly working with and printing large, complex and memory-intensive documents.

The Server uses a special Network Operating System (NOS) that allows it to share resources with the Clients. NetWare and Windows NT/2000 are two current popular Network Operating Systems. This provides the Server with its most important benefit: administration can all be done from a single location/source.

Client/Server networks are often used in larger organizations in which perhaps many users might need access to the network at any one time.

Peer-to-peer

In a Peer-to-peer network, there's no single Server PC that controls who does what, where and when. Here, every PC on the LAN is both a Client and a Server. Also, every PC can have direct access to every other PC on the LAN. The big advantages of a Peer-to-peer LAN are that no single PC needs to be reserved as the file Server and the required network software comes built into Microsoft Windows.

Peer-to-peer networks can provide an ideal simple solution for small networks of say up to 10 PCs. However, if your funds allow, the more powerful and expensive Client/server network would almost certainly run much more smoothly. Microsoft Windows (95/98/Me/XP/NT/2000) has built in Peer-to-peer networking and it is this networking system that we will cover in this chapter.

Network interface cards

Network cable connectors

4-input network hub

Microsoft Windows also includes Dial-up networking, providing an ideal modem-based method for someone working from home to communicate with an organization's LAN to retrieve data.

An Uninterruptible Power Supply or UPS is an essential component of any serious network. A UPS can protect against power fluctuations and sudden mains supply power failures.

Typical components that make up a network

It's surprising what goes in to make up a small, typical, basic computer network or LAN today. Consider:

• File Server/PCs plus perhaps mirrored Servers

• Network Operating System software

• Workstations

• Workstation operating system software and applications

• Printers, CD-ROM drives and modems

• Network Interface Cards (NICs) (see page 129)

• Network hub(s)

• Network cabling (if not using infrared or wireless)

• Data backup equipment and software

• Backup power supply (UPS) (see Hot Tip in margin)

Network hubs

A hub is simply an electronic box designed to accept the connecting cables (or electronic signals) from all the PCs on the network. A hub is a central routing station for your data. It ensures that each PC is able to communicate with all others connected to the hub.

Network hub from 3Com

Gigabit Ethernet is a recently developed network standard that enables data to be transferred at a rate of 1,000Mbps (1,000 million bits per second)!

A hub typically accepts up to 5, 8, 12 or 16 devices and if your network expands, you can typically daisy-chain hubs together to allow more devices to be connected.

Currently, Token Ring networks can move data at a rate of 4–16Mbps. This is achieved by passing a virtual 'token' from PC to PC. As the token arrives, it collects the information and passes it on to the next PC, until the data reaches its destination.

Three network hubs from Netgear allowing 4, 8, and 16 devices to be networked together

Network layouts (topologies)

Most networks apply one of the three following layouts:

- **Bus:** here, each PC is connected by a cable to the 'main data highway' or bus.

- **Star:** each PC is connected to a 'central' hub. The hub helps route data to the desired PC. The Star network layout is currently the most popular method used today, and this is the type of network examined in the following pages.

- **Ring:** also known as Token Ring. Here, each PC is connected to the 'next' PC in line and the 'last' PC in the chain connects to the 'first' PC to form a complete 'ring'.

Choosing a network card

What is a Network Interface Card (NIC)?

A network card determines how information flows between the PC and the network. Each PC connected to a network must have a Network Interface Card installed on its motherboard. In non-infrared/wireless varieties, the network cable then plugs into the appropriate socket on the NIC.

Determining what type of cards to buy

First, make sure the card you choose is an Ethernet network card. Typically, network cards are available from established makers like 3Com, IBM, Intel Pro and Systemax. For Pentium-type PCs, ideally, choose a PCI-type network card rather than the older, slower ISA type. For a notebook PC, equivalent PC Card network cards are also available.

Almost all Network Interface Cards are designed either for use on Ethernet or Token ring networks. When you buy a NIC, make sure that it is compatible with the type of network you're creating.

Also, if you're buying NICs, cables and a hub separately, make sure all NICs support the type of cable/connectors you're using.

Most current NICs are available in two speeds:

- 10Mbps – megabits per second – also known as 10BaseT. Now somewhat dated

- 100Mbps, also known as 100BaseT: the current standard

Token Ring Network cards can also use a DB9 (9-pin D-shaped connector) or an RJ45-type connector.

For most users – even for linking only two PCs – I recommend you try to choose network cards and hubs that transmit at 100Mbps to help transfer information as fast as possible around the network.

Network card connectors

Ethernet cards use:

- RJ45 connectors (for 10BaseT cables). RJ45 connectors look similar to standard telephone plugs

- A BNC connector (for Thinnet coaxial cable)

- A DB15 connector (D-shaped 15-pin used for ThickNet coaxial cable – rarely used nowadays)

- A combination of all three above included

Coaxial network cable with connectors from Videk Cabling

RJ45 network cable with connectors

Netgear PCI Network Interface Card

In the following pages, where we have mentioned 'double-click', if you're using Windows 98/ Me/XP/2000 and have configured this action as a single-click, then that applies instead.

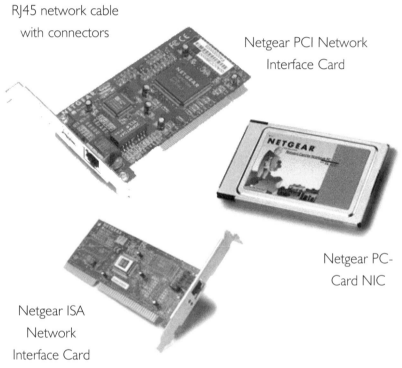

Usually, it's OK to mix different brands of Ethernet Network cards provided they're all Ethernet-compatible.

Netgear ISA Network Interface Card

Netgear PC-Card NIC

Setting up your network in the following pages

Within the following few pages, we're going to illustrate the steps required to set up a network using a Peer-to-peer network such as that built into Windows (95/98/Me/XP/NT/2000).

The procedure is a little intense: getting a group of PCs to 'talk' to each other can be one of the most complex or the most simple of tasks, depending on your particular set up and configuration. If you've not installed a network before, complete each step before going on to the following step, allow plenty of time to complete each task and try not to be interrupted until you're finished.

Installing a network card in a Plug-and-Play (PnP) system

All new network cards should be fully Plug-and-Play (PnP)-compatible. Installing into a PnP-compatible PC is usually straightforward as Microsoft Windows should install the necessary drivers for you. In our example below, we've used a central hub-based (star) network with RJ45 connectors. Always read the maker's instructions that come with your network cards or network kit. To physically install your network cards, start by switching off all PCs and unplugging their power leads. Then, remove their outer covers and perform the steps below.

If you're using an older non-Plug-and-Play PC system, you'll probably have to manually install the network card, rather than let Microsoft Windows install it for you.

After completing step 3, Microsoft Windows may prompt you to enter a user name and password.

1 Insert the first PCI network card into a spare slot: consider the guidelines on page 85 for installing any expansion card. Repeat the procedure and install the remaining cards.

2 Insert one end of the network lead into the first card and the other end into the appropriate socket on the hub. Repeat with the leads from the other network cards.

3 Plug in the power supply to the hub and switch on. Then switch on all PCs in the network – the slowest ones first.

Once you switch on the PCs, watch the screens (see the lower Don't Forget Tip in the margin). Depending on your version of Microsoft Windows and your particular set up, Windows may automatically install the correct software drivers for you. Or you may be prompted to insert the disk containing the drivers that may have come with the cards. If not, further guidelines are provided overleaf. Finally, you'll need to switch off and reboot each PC.

Working with passwords

Once the network is set up and operational, usually you have to enter a user name and password to gain access to information on the network. When trying to devise a password, avoid using any references, words or numbers that people can link to you. Often, the best password can be created using a special character (like #) to link a word and a number sequence (like: topf#384).

In order for a Peer-to-peer network to work in Windows, key information must be installed. With most recent PCs, Microsoft Windows normally installs and sets up each network card automatically. If not, you can install these settings manually. Consider the following guidelines.

Once your network cards have been installed and your network is operating normally, you can double-click on the Network Neighborhood icon on the Windows desktop to see a list of all PCs on the network. Then, simply double-click on a desired PC to gain access to its folders and files.

1 Open the Windows Control Panel, then double-click Network.

2 Click the Configuration tab. Usually, at least five or six key entries should have been added here, including Client for Microsoft Networks, Client for NetWare Networks, the icon representing the relevant NIC, IPX/SPX-compatible Protocol, and NetBEUI. If not, you need to identify why. See your Windows Help documentation on networks.

To provide access to files and share printers over a Windows network, choose the 'File And Printer Sharing' option. However, if you're using an Internet-based network, make sure you have set up additional security or disable this option to prevent unauthorized access to your files while online.

3 In the Primary Network Logon box, usually you need to choose Client for Microsoft Networks.

4 Click the Identification tab, then type a brief name (under 15 characters, no spaces) for your PC. Press the TAB key.

5 Type a name for the workgroup: all the PCs you want to network must have the same workgroup name. Example: you could enter 'Office' or 'Home_office' (without the quotes); note: no spaces. Press the TAB key. Click OK.

You can also simplify the business of sharing hard drives, printers, modems, CD-ROM drives and other resources on a LAN. See your Windows documentation for precise details of how to 'map' network drives and 'share resources'.

6 Restart/reboot the computer.

7 Repeat steps 1–6 for every other PC in your network.

Testing your LAN

Now you're ready to confirm whether you have set up each PC in the LAN correctly. Shut down and restart all PCs in the LAN. When all the PCs have started Windows normally, go to each PC and double-click the Network Neighborhood icon. In each Network Neighborhood window, you should see an icon for each PC in the LAN. Double-click each icon to view the relevant files and folders. Well done. Congratulations!

Modems and fast Internet connections

Modems allow us to connect to other computers anywhere. ISDN terminal adaptors do the same thing but much faster, and there are still newer technologies emerging that promise an explosion of cheaper global communications. In this chapter, we examine these themes and provide some guidelines to consider when buying, installing and setting up this equipment.

Covers

Chapter Sixteen

Introducing the modem

The word modem is derived from MOdulation and DEModulation. The purpose of a modem is twofold. Firstly, information is coded (modulated) at the source end by converting digital signals from the PC into analogue signals suitable for the telephone network. Secondly, at the destination end, the information is decoded (demodulated) to convert the analogue signals back into the kind of digital signals a PC understands.

Modems, both internal and external, are now available in serveral varieties – as examined in more detail on the facing page.

Dynalink internal
PCI card modem

A 'bit' is the smallest piece of information that a PC can use. It has two states: 1 (high) or 0 (low). Modem speed is measured in thousands of bits per second (Kbps) or baud, although these two don't strictly mean quite the same thing.

Modem speeds and standards

One of the most important modem specifications is speed, measured in thousands of bits per second (Kbps). As phone lines were originally only developed to carry voice signals, conventional land-based phone lines are usually limited to an absolute maximum 56Kbps modem speed.

The older 28.8Kbps and 33.6Kbps modems have now largely been superseded by faster 56Kbps models. Likewise, the two incompatible 56Kbps standards of a few years ago – X2 and K56Flex – have also been superseded by the V.90 – the one true 56Kbps standard.

At the time of writing, the slightly faster V.92 standard is just starting to appear. However, few Internet Service Providers support it. Most support the V.90 standard and are waiting to see if there's enough demand to justify the extra costs involved in supporting V.92.

V.90 was developed to help merge the K56Flex and X2 competing 56K standards and reduce the amount of confusion caused by having two conflicting methods to address the same problem.

Types of modem

Modems now come in four main types:

- Internal

- External

- PC Card (formerly PCMCIA).

- Software modems (also called: WinModems)

Internal modems

An internal modem is a plug-in card that fits into a spare PCI (or even ISA) expansion slot. Benefits: an internal modem requires no casing or power supply, does not take up desk space and doesn't need extra cables, so prices tend to be lower than for external models. Drawbacks: an internal modem does generate some extra heat and doesn't directly provide status and call-progress indicator lights.

Some modems actually come as part of a motherboard. The advantage here is that you don't need to use a slot or perform any additional set up tasks.

External modems

An external modem is often the easiest to set up. It simply plugs into a PC just like a printer, using the serial, parallel, SCSI, or USB ports, depending on the specific model. You also don't need an expansion slot, and can easily move an external modem from PC to PC. External modems also usually provide a range of call-progress and status-indicator lights. External modems tend to cost more than internal equivalents, to cover casing and power-supply/data cables.

Besides modem and ISDN, other data transfer systems are continually being developed and improved, including: cable TV, optical fibre, satellite links and ADSL/ RADSL (pages 143/144).

PC Card modems

For notebook users, PC Card modems are usually about the size of a credit card and contain extremely high-density component packing. Drawback: fits only in a PC Card slot.

Software modems: saving cost and reducing power

These latest modems – popular in notebook PCs – actually use special software routines to make up a modem, with most of the number-crunching being performed by the PC's CPU or through a Digital Signal Processor (DSP) chip. A WinModem is a type of software modem that in order to function relies on Microsoft Windows being present. This is clearly a drawback if you intend to use another operating system.

Choosing a modem

When deciding which modem to purchase, there are several important factors you should consider:

- The **type of modem:** internal, external, PC Card, or software modem.

- **Modem speed:** *the most important specification*. The current speed to aim for is 56Kbps using the true V.90 standard. However, remember your ISP needs to support the V.90 standard.

Modem speeds are measured using the V-standards. The main V-standards include: V.21 (300bps); V.22 (1,200bps); V.22bis (2,400bps); V.32bis (14,400bps); V.34 (28,800 and 33,600bps); and V.90 (56,000bps) – the current standard.

- **Compatibility:** make sure your modem is compatible with the Hayes command set and approved for use on your telephone network (for the UK: BABT-approved). Note: it's illegal to use a non-BABT-approved modem on UK telephone lines.

- **Software:** to drive your modem. No modem will work without appropriate software, which allows you to dial numbers, control the modem and send and receive files and (optionally) faxes. Windows 95/98/Me/XP/NT/2000 includes built-in dialler software.

Most modems today should also be able to transmit and receive faxes as well as data. Some can also provide additional facilities like telephone-answering; microphone/speaker setup for simultaneous voice transmission and reception; and even built-in configuration for video-conferencing!

- To handle data faster than about 9,600bps reliably, usually most modems need a **high-speed serial card or interface** using a 16550 or 16650 UART chip, although for software modems, Digital Signal Processor chips may be used instead. Also, usually, new motherboards should come with the serial interface built in.

- **Error-correction:** essential to provide speedy data throughput. Current popular protocols include MNP 1–4 and the Hayes V- series.

- **Data-compression:** MNP5 and preferably V.42bis can considerably help boost modem speed.

- **Fax capability:** If you want to send faxes using your modem, ensure your modem meets Group III fax protocol.

Installing a hardware modem

Ideally use a PC with a fast Pentium CPU; 64Mb or greater of RAM; a fast video card; a 3Gb or larger hard drive; a quad-speed or faster CD-ROM drive; a SoundBlaster-compatible sound card; a 17" or larger colour display monitor; and with Windows 95/98/Me/XP/NTv4/2000 .

Installing an internal modem

Consider the guidelines below.

Half-duplex mode allows data to be transmitted or received in both directions, but only one or the other direction at any one time. Full-duplex mode allows transmission and reception of data simultaneously. The V.90 standard uses Full-duplex mode.

1 Switch off your PC and carefully remove its casing.

2 You may need to configure the modem to the Com port you're using; read your modem's documentation.

3 Remove the blanking plate from the slot you want to use. Carefully push the modem card into the desired slot and secure with the mounting screw. Note: guidelines on page 85.

4 Refit the PC's casing and switch on. Windows should automatically detect the new modem and install it. If not, you can use the Add New Hardware icon in the Control Panel.

Installing an external modem

If you install a Plug-and-Play modem into a Plug-and-Play PC, Microsoft Windows should install and configure the modem for you automatically. However, sometimes, Windows may prompt you to insert a disk containing specific drivers.

1 Switch off both the PC and the modem.

2 Make the physical connections as described in your modem's installation guide. Connect the computer's serial port or USB port to the modem; refer to the documentation.

3 If your modem includes a telephone loop-through connector, connect your phone to the appropriate socket.

4 Insert the telephone cable linking the modem with the telephone wall socket.

5 Switch on the modem and the PC. Windows should install your modem software as examined on the following page.

Installing modem software

Once the modem hardware is installed in or connected to the PC, you can easily update Windows to acknowledge the new modem. If the modem is an external model, switch it on now. If the modem is an internal model, the modem will switch on when you switch on the PC. Therefore, switch the PC on now also.

If Windows detects the new modem, the appropriate software drivers will be automatically installed for you. If not, you can install the correct driver by carrying out the steps below. Even if the drivers were installed automatically, you can still verify the correct installation by following the steps below:

1   Make sure you have your Windows CD-ROM or floppy disks close by, plus optionally an installation disk if one came with your modem.

2   Click the Windows Start button, followed by the Settings command, followed by the Control Panel command.

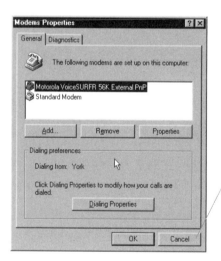

3   In the Control Panel, double-click the Modems icon. If Windows has already set up this modem, the Modems Properties dialog box appears. Click the Cancel button.

If Windows has not set up the modem, the Install New Modem wizard box appears. Go to step 4.

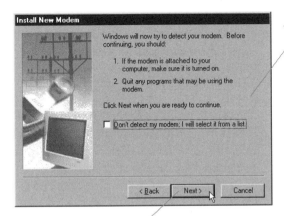

4 The opening dialog box from the Install New Modem wizard appears when your modem has not been set up in Windows.

5 Click the Next button.

6 Follow the remaining onscreen instructions to install your modem. If Windows does not have the correct driver for

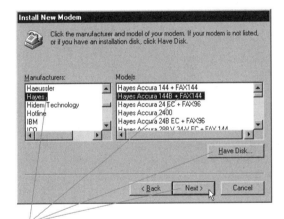

your modem, at the appropriate time you can click the 'Have Disk' button and use the floppy disk that came with your modem.

7 When finished, close down and restart Windows. Then return to the Windows desktop and try out your modem using your preferred online access software. Note: you need to set up your online access software to work with your new modem also.

Installing an ISDN terminal adaptor

The telephone system was originally designed to handle voice-based information only, so using a modem to move data is sometimes slow and unreliable. The ISDN or Integrated Services Digital Network, however, was designed specifically to transfer voice, data and video signals.

The big benefits of ISDN over the modem are speed (up to 128Kbps) and quality (entirely digital, so less interference). The main disadvantage, at present, is cost: ISDN is expensive unless you send a lot of data regularly and can recoup your costs.

How does ISDN work?

Depending on which country you live in, to have an ISDN connection installed, you may need to be located within about 5.5km of an ISDN telephone exchange. Speak to your Internet Service Provider and supplier for more information about ISDN options available for your area.

Currently, basic-rate ISDN can provide three channels in which to transfer voice, data and video information: one at 16Kbps and two at 64Kbps. The voice and data information can be combined to provide 128Kbps – much faster than even the fastest modems. Alternatively, for corporate users, the premium-rate ISDN service may be more suitable, using optical fibre and providing up to 30 channels.

pace ISDN TA

An ISDN system doesn't use a modem; instead, you need an ISDN terminal adaptor for each PC linked to the ISDN system. Currently, ISDN terminal adaptors are generally a little more expensive than some modems.

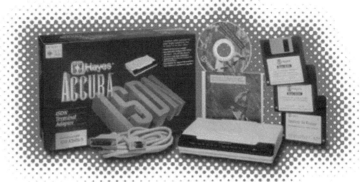

You also need the appropriate ISDN software and possibly an upgraded serial card. Speak to your computer supplier to identify your exact requirements. ISDN adaptors are currently available from well-known companies like Pace, BT, US Robotics, Hayes, Intel, Elsa, and others. Lastly, remember of course that you also need an ISDN account.

ISDN and the Internet

One point to bear in mind if you plan to surf the Internet using ISDN: there's a speed advantage over a modem only if your Internet Service Provider (ISP) fully supports ISDN.

So if you're considering ISDN, confirm with your ISP exactly what ISDN services they provide. Also, compare prices, as these costs can vary considerably.

US Robotics ISDN Terminal Adaptor card 1

ISDN solution from Hayes

Speeding up with ADSL

Modems and ISDN both have major drawbacks: principally, one is slow and although the other is faster, it's often too expensive for most ordinary users. During the next few years, both ISDN2 and BT Home Highway may become outdated by one or more of the emerging technologies described below.

Some of these technologies have been available for several years, but only now are they beginning to offer great benefits.

Key components include price, speed and quality! Arguably, several technologies could possibly offer a better way to communicate over the Internet, including:

The longer you are connected to the Internet, the greater the security risk to your data. Therefore, regularly re-evaluate your Internet security and take the necessary steps to strengthen your defences. For more information, see the excellent Gibson Research Corporation website at: www.grc.com/

- Direct-broadcast by Satellite (DBS)

- Cable modem communications

- Asymmetric Digital Subscriber Line (ADSL)

Direct Broadcast by Satellite (DBS)

A DBS system can *download* files and information to your home up to a maximum speed of about 400Kbps. *Uploading* (to an Internet Service Provider), however, uses the 'standard' modem speed – in practice, about 30-40Kbps.

Even though the upload speed is much slower, the overall efficiency of DBS can be considered to be a combination of both the upload and download speeds. DBS is therefore especially suited to users who want to download many large files regularly.

Using a cable modem

A cable modem allows you fast access (8Mbps) to the Internet using the same type of cable that attaches to a cable television set. Your local cable TV company may offer fast Internet access using this method (however, watch ADSL developments closely to save money!).

ADSL and RADSL: options and possibilities

ADSL is arguably one of the most exciting of the new technologies set to provide amazing possibilities for individuals across the globe.

So what's all the excitement about? Answer: ADSL can offer amazingly fast connection speeds. Internet Service Provider-to-user (downstream) speeds of about 1.5Mbps–8.4Mbps may be possible, and user- to-ISP (upstream) speeds of 16Kbps–640Kbps are available.

However, in practice, ADSL connection speeds can vary somewhat depending on several conditions including how many other users are currently using a line.

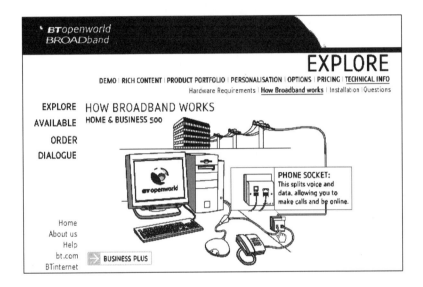

BT at www.btopenworld.com/ are already offering a range of ADSL options tailored for home users, and small and larger business users. For example, BT's Home 500 package offers maximum connection rates of 500Kbps downstream and 250Kbps upstream – even these speeds may improve in time. Compare these kinds of speeds with the much slower 56Kbps modem!

So what does this service cost? Currently, to use BT Home 500, you'll need to part with about £40 per month and a £150 installation fee, both prices excluding VAT.

What is amazing is that ADSL provides this high speed Internet access using the standard twisted pair telephone lines we use today, with few modifications being required to existing telephone systems.

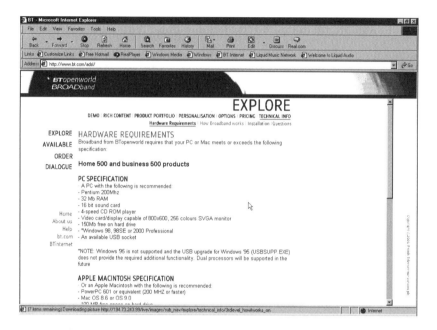

To get ADSL, ask your ISP to confirm that you can receive ADSL at your current location – typically, you'll need to be situated within about 3.5km of an ADSL-compatible exchange. If you can receive it, then you'll need a special card which simply plugs into the decoder box and an ISP that supports the desired ADSL package.

Another option to emerge recently is Rate Adaptive Digital Subscriber Line (RADSL) – a kind of enhanced ADSL which promises to offer ADSL-type Internet speeds for users who may be situated too far from an ADSL-compatible exchange, or just outside of the ADSL geographical limit.

Faster Internet access can mean less time spent online, providing added savings. Alternatively, more efficient, better response could result in increased usage as users could simply do more in the same amount of time. Only time will tell.

PC cases and power supplies

PC cases come in a wide variety of shapes, sizes and styles. Most cases come with a power supply. However, you'll need to match the power supply and the case to your system. This chapter covers what you need to know when purchasing a case and power supply and how to deal with the sometimes tricky topic of notebook PC batteries.

Covers

Chapter Seventeen

Replacing a desktop PC case

Caution: buy PC cases/power supplies only from a reputable supplier. Also, make sure the power supply has the CE mark.

PC cases and accessories

Most new desktop PCs now use the ATX case design. An ATX power supply requires an ATX case and motherboard. Some case makers provide only the power supply. Others also provide a range of useful screws, cables, and connectors.

Power supplies: establishing the wattage

Make sure the case/power supply is compatible with your motherboard. The new ATX-form motherboard requires an ATX-compatible case/power supply. However, some motherboards will accept both the old AT power supply connectors and the newer ATX. Check with your supplier.

AC mains voltage enters a power supply and is converted to several different lower DC voltage levels. When you buy a new case, usually a power supply comes built in. Caution: make sure the wattage rating in the new power supply is the same as or larger than your existing power supply/case.

Replacing an entire PC case

First, switch off the PC and disconnect the PC from the mains supply. Next, carefully remove the PC case cover. Consider the following guidelines.

Surge protectors (also called suppressors) are useful to have connected to your PC system. These help protect a PC from power surges that sometimes occur – mainly during thunder storms.

1 Note down all the connections plugged into the motherboard and which cards are plugged into which slots.

2 Gently unplug all connections to the motherboard, remove all plug-in cards and carefully store each in a safe place.

3 Remove the motherboard as described on page 24. Remove the hard drive from its mounting cage. Remove floppy drive, tape drives, CD-ROM/DVD drives and any other drives attached. Note which screws are used with which item.

4 With the new case disconnected from the mains supply, carefully refit each item removed from the old case into the new case.

5 Before switching on, thoroughly check your reconnections with your notes to ensure all connections are correct.

Notebook PC batteries

Let's take a close look at the different types of notebook PC battery available. Notebook batteries come in four main types:

- **Nickel Cadmium (NiCad)**: oldest design of the four. Not many of these are still working. Biggest drawback: effective battery life may be reduced by up to 40% if not fully discharged before recharging.

- **Nickel Metal-Hydride (NiMH)**: these batteries last considerably longer – in fact the charge–recharge cycle can sometimes reach 500 times!

- **Lithium-Ion (Li-Ion)**: a lightweight metal, Lithium-Ion represents the most popular notebook battery type today and the most expensive of the three listed so far.

- **Lithium-Ion Polymer**: one of the latest lightweight designs, this type of battery is much lighter than the Lithium-Ion type and keeps its charge for considerably longer. Again, 500 charge–recharge cycles are usually possible with the battery – clearly it is set to become the leader.

To help maximise the life of a battery usually, aim to fully discharge the battery before recharging. However, always read the appropriate document-ation first.

Some batteries (in particular NiCad- and NiMH- types) can display a kind of false memory effect. After some use, a battery may not recharge fully as the false memory effect may indicate that it is already fully charged.

Inspiron 5000 BATTERY MODULE

P/N: 083KV or P/N: 2127U

Replacing a motherboard battery

How does a PC remember the date when we switch it off? Answer: by maintaining power to a special chip (the ROM BIOS) and keeping its associated electronic clock (Real Time Clock) working correctly.

Sometimes, this power is provided by a special chip that has its own battery built in (NVRAM chip). Other motherboards use a special electronic component – a high-value capacitor – to store the required tiny amount of electricity needed to maintain the BIOS settings and clock.

When changing an RTC/NVRAM chip, before removing the old chip, first identify pin 1 (usually, the chip may have a marker or dot next to pin 1). Then, after carefully removing the old chip, install the new one, making sure you fit pin 1 to socket pin 1.

With a capacitor-based motherboard, the capacitor is recharged automatically every time the PC is powered up. Other motherboards simply use a special small battery.

Real Time Clock (RTC)/NVRAM batteries

Lithium is currently the preferred substance used in PC motherboard batteries. The electronic chips containing a tiny lithium battery often have an effective life of about 10 years! If you need to replace the RTC/NVRAM chip, usually you only need to carefully unplug/remove the old chip and refit a new one (but see Beware Tip in the margin and the instructions below first).

When replacing the PC battery/ chip, first make sure you obtain the correct one.
WARNING: EXPLOSION RISK: connect or resolder the battery using the correct polarity.

Conventional backup batteries for PCs usually come as a 3.6V, 4.5V or 6V cell. You can easily identify when a battery is nearing the end of its life: almost every time you switch on your PC, you may need to manually re-enter the date and time to update the clock.

Replacing the battery/chip

Before removing the battery or chip according to the maker's instructions, enter your PC's BIOS SETUP program and record all its details: this is a precaution. See Chapters 2 and 5 for guidelines on displaying BIOS settings or refer to your PC's documentation.

Then, quickly change the battery or chip (note the BEWARE notes in the margin): sometimes, the BIOS may maintain its settings for a few minutes (a type of memory effect). But if you're unlucky, simply re-enter the recorded BIOS information afterwards.

Keyboard and mouse

Every PC needs an input device which allows you to control what happens. The keyboard and mouse are the two most important input devices. However, other options are now available. This chapter examines input devices and the factors involved when you upgrade.

Covers

Chapter Eighteen

Choosing a keyboard

Several types of keyboard are now available. Most use the popular QWERTY-type keyboard layout providing 101 keys (102 to cater for language differences) or 104 keys to handle the new commands in Windows 95/98/Me/XP/NT/2000.

Keyboard connectors

Traditionally, three main types of keyboard connector are used. Most newer ATX-type motherboards either use the 6-pin mini-DIN socket, also known as a PS/2 (IBM) connector, or a Universal Serial Bus (USB) connector. Some older motherboards may use a 5-pin DIN connector. These connectors are not mutually compatible, so make sure you buy the correct keyboard.

If your keyboard has a connector which is not compatible with your motherboard, your computer dealer may sell a special adaptor to remedy the problem.

Keyboard settings – sensitivity and response – can be changed using the Windows Control Panel.

Windows keyboard

The Windows keyboard adds three extra keys to the standard 101/102-key keyboard, to allow for Windows-specific functions. This is ideal for touch typists who don't want to operate the mouse from time to time, as all the Windows mouse functions are available from the Windows keyboard.

The three new keys include: two Windows Logo keys, one each side of the SPACEBAR – these keys open the Windows Start menu – and the Context Menu or Application key, which is situated to the right of the SPACEBAR and opens a context-specific menu. Remember, it's not essential to have a 'Windows' keyboard to use Microsoft Windows: many people still use a standard 101- or 102-key keyboard.

'Natural' and ergonomic keyboards

Several 'natural' keyboard designs have emerged in recent years. Some have been redesigned, changing the shape of the keyboard and providing wrist rests, whilst still keeping the essential key layout the same. The Alps keyboard and the Microsoft Natural keyboard are examples of these. Some have a 'soft' key action; others have a more positive mechanical action.

The now more rare Dvorak keyboard takes a completely different approach. August Dvorak, who patented his design in 1936, arranged the keys so that the most often used letters are placed within easier reach at the centre of the keyboard. This approach allegedly makes touch-typing more comfortable. Claims have also been made that Dvorak keyboards can reduce instances of RSI.

The Trackball keyboard

A Trackball keyboard saves space by including a mouse, with the Trackball and its microswitches performing the functions of a mouse, and so can minimise the amount of required hand movement. Usually, the Trackball is sited in place of the arrow keys on a standard 101- (or 102-) key keyboard.

A buying checklist

Some people prefer a soft, dampened click of the keys. Others prefer to feel and hear a definite click when a key is pressed. Take some time in choosing your keyboard; consider the following guidelines:

- Which keyboard design do you prefer?

- Key action: do you prefer a hard or soft response?

- Are the keys spaced apart adequately?

- Do the key tops wobble too much?

- Does the keyboard have a solid backplate?

- Do the keyboard backplate grips hold the keyboard in place adequately on a desk?

A keyboard wrist rest can lift up your wrists slightly to help provide additional comfort – especially valuable if, like me, you spend many hours touch-typing.

Sometimes, a keyboard can collect a build-up of small dust particles trapped under the keys. One of the best ways to remove these is to spray the area with canned compressed air using the supplied straw. However, do switch off your PC and spray away from your eyes.

Replacing a mouse

Most mice come with two buttons as required by Microsoft Windows, with the left button usually configured for most actions, and the right mouse button reserved for special actions or short-cuts. Most ATX-type motherboards now use an IBM PS/2-type mouse connector – a 6-pin mini DIN plug – or you can use a USB mouse, or even a wireless solution.

In addition to mice with the arguably more common DB9 and PS/2 connectors, mice are now available in several forms including the Universal Serial Bus (USB) connection and even wireless infrared. Soon, you may also be able to buy a mouse and keyboard that uses wireless Bluetooth technology too.

Other pointing devices

Several other types of pointing device have also emerged, including: the Trackball (page 151), the Glidepoint and the Trackpoint. The Glidepoint is popular in notebook PCs – you simply slide your finger over a small touch-sensitive pad to move the pointer on the screen, and tap the pad to make a choice.

The Trackpoint consists of a small rubberised knob sited between the G, H and B keys on a standard 101/102-key keyboard. By applying directional finger pressure to the protruding knob, a user can move the pointer on the screen in the same way as a mouse. The Trackpoint helps save desk space, reduce finger movement, and it has no moving parts and so does not accumulate dirt.

Mouse mats usually come either with a smooth or a textured surface. A smooth surface demands less effort from the mouse hand or wrist. Also, use a mouse mat to slow down the build up of dirt and foreign matter on the rubber-coated ball and the rollers against which the rubber ball moves.

The IntelliMouse

The Microsoft IntelliMouse includes an additional wheel sited between the two buttons that is useful in specially designed software. The wheel can also be used as a third mouse button.

Scroll More Easily

Zoom Efficiently

Raised Back Fits Your Hand

Using the index finger to operate the small wheel provides an extra level of speed and control when scrolling and web browsing, and you can even 'zoom in' to images and text. IntelliMouse v2.0 software also includes the 'ClickLock' function which allows you to drag items without having to hold down the primary mouse button – a useful addition!

Adjusting your mouse settings

When you install Windows, default mouse settings are automatically applied to your mouse. However, sometimes you may want to change these settings: for example, you may be left-handed, or the double-click speed may be incorrect. Alternatively, you may have upgraded your mouse to one of the new breed, in which case you may need to tell Windows about your new mouse. To change your mouse parameters, carry out the steps below.

The options available in your version of Windows or operating system may differ slightly from the steps listed on this page.

If you want to create more free space on your desk, you can opt for a cordless mouse. Movement of the mouse sends electronic signals to the PC. You will, though, need to replace the mouse battery regularly.

1 On the Windows desktop, click the Start button, followed by Settings, then Control Panel.

2 In the Control Panel, double-click the Mouse icon to display the Mouse Properties dialog box.

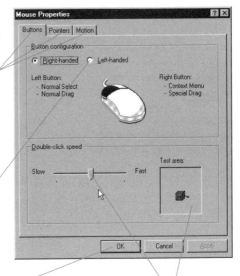

4 (Optional) To change the mouse pointer shapes or the motion speed, click the appropriate tab, and make your desired changes.

5 (Optional) To change to a left-handed mouse, click here.

6 To confirm your new settings, click OK.

3 (Optional) To slow down or speed up the double-click speed, drag the slider to the desired position. You can try your new setting in the Test area.

Maintaining your mouse

A mouse is probably one of the most used components of any modern PC. Working in Windows involves performing a lot of mouse operations. Consequently, over time, signs of wear and tear may emerge.

Logitech MouseMan

The mouse pointer or cursor may move erratically when you move the mouse, and sometimes you may have to repeat an action to move the pointer to a desired position (see margin Tips). To clean your mouse, carry out the following steps.

Take care with isopropyl alcohol. Always follow the directions given by the supplier. Don't touch your eyes while using it and always wash your hands thoroughly after use.

To avoid jerky mouse movements and reduce stress on your mouse hand and wrist, regularly clean the slightly raised platforms on the base of your mouse that slide over the mouse mat.

1 Close down any open applications. Then also close Microsoft Windows and switch off your PC.

2 Turn the mouse upside-down, loosen the mouse ball cover and remove it. Or remove any screws that may be holding the cover in place.

3 Cover the hole exposing the mouse ball and turn the mouse right side up. The mouse ball should drop into your hand.

4 Examine the ball for dust and dirt stuck to its surface. You can clean the ball in warm soapy water, or use a contact cleaner like isopropyl alcohol. If you use isopropyl alcohol, follow the manufacturer's safety precautions (see margin). When complete, dry the ball thoroughly.

5 Next, visually examine the two plastic rollers or wheels. If there is dirt on them, you could try blowing out the dust with canned compressed air, or alternatively, gently clean the rollers with a cotton bud soaked in isopropyl alcohol or soapy water.

6 Before refitting the ball and ball cover, allow the rollers and ball to dry thoroughly.

Working with external devices

In this chapter, we examine the four most important add-on devices: printers, scanners, digital cameras and handheld PCs. When used in partnership with a desktop computer, these valuable devices help provide a new amazing level of power and flexibility to a PC system.

Covers

Chapter Nineteen

Connecting a printer to your PC

Introduction to printers

Both black and white and colour PC printers are available in several types, including: laser, inkjet and more rarely dot-matrix.

The quality of printed output is determined mainly by the printer resolution, measured in dots per inch (dpi).

Most printers for desktop and portable computers today are either laser or inkjet-based. When evaluating which type of printer to buy, also consider the cost of ink or toner. Why? A low-priced printer might mean higher costs of toner or ink.

Printer speed is measured in pages per minute (ppm). Although a higher printing speed provides faster output, if the document you're printing is complex – contains images as well as text – printing speed slows. Sometimes, you can add more memory to a printer to help speed up printing.

The higher the dpi, the sharper the printed output. So a 1200 dpi printer provides better quality output than a 600 dpi printer – although do remember that the paper chosen can also affect image quality.

Key point: if you want the best possible printed output, choose a good quality smooth paper.

Most printers today provide at least 600 dpi – ideal if you mostly print text-dominated documents. If the quality of printed images is more important, you may consider a 1200 dpi printer to be preferable.

hp LaserJet 1100

designed for

- Individual business users in any size office who want to print laser quality documents. They need true laser print quality, speed and paper handling at their desk

- The HP LaserJet 1100 prints quick professional - looking documents at your desk. It is easy to set up and use, and extremely reliable. You can also upgrade it to a printer that copies with the copier/scanner attachment.

hp LaserJet 2200

designed for

- for business professionals and small workgroups in any sized office, seeking reliable and efficient document management solutions, the HP LaserJet 2200 delivers superior performance, increased productivity and exceptional versatility.

Sometimes, you may also see printer resolution described using two sets of figures – for example: 600 x 600 dpi. This approach states how many dots are printed across and down in a single square inch (600 x 600 = 360,000 dots).

Installing your printer

To print a document from your PC, your PC must first be set up to work with your particular printer. Consider the guidelines below.

If you have problems getting a new printer to print correctly, the problem is in one or more of three areas: the printer, the connection, or the setup in Windows. To confirm that the printer is working correctly, disconnect it from the PC and run the 'self-test' routine or print a test page. Check your printer documentation for details.

Printing a large or complex document using a Microsoft Windows Peer-to-peer network may take quite a while, display errors, or may not even print completely, especially if other users on the network are also working with similarly large or complex documents at the same time. One answer: consider investing in a Client/Server-based network. Get professional advice first.

1 You connect the printer to your PC as directed in the instructions, using either a physical printer cable that links either to the printer socket or to a USB socket on the PC, or you may opt for a printer that uses a wireless technology such as radio waves or infrared.

2 Your PC needs to have installed a small software program known as the printer driver. Usually, in Microsoft Windows, when you connect any new device, Windows attempts to recognize the kind of device you're installing and tries to install the correct driver. Sometimes, if Windows cannot find the correct driver from its own database, it may ask you to insert a disk containing the latest driver, provided by the printer maker.

3 Install the printer driver as directed in the maker's instructions.

4 After the printer driver is installed, you'll probably need to restart your PC to ensure Microsoft Windows is updated to include the new printer.

5 Most printers allow a test page to be printed. To confirm that your printer is installed properly and functioning correctly, print a test page. A successfully printed test page ensures that the printer and PC can communicate correctly.

With earlier versions of Windows, you may need to install the printer driver manually. Check your Windows documentation.

Adding a scanner

Scanner basics

A scanner performs the opposite role to a printer: it accepts a printed page or image and converts it into an electronic form. Scanners come in three main types: handheld, sheet-fed and flat bed. Most scanners today are of the flat bed variety: these allow you to scan pages of a book or an A4-size report without causing any damage to the document.

To scan text for use in word processing software, remember you'll also need Optical Character Recognition (OCR) software – which may come bundled with a new scanner.

Scanner makers often provide additional bundled software packages with a new scanner, so you may not need to buy any extra graphics software.

For best scan results, always keep the glass surface on which you place your documents clean and dry. Keep a soft dry cloth handy to quickly wipe the surface immediately before scanning.

Like printers, scan quality is measured in dots per inch (dpi), in black and white or colour. A connection to the PC can be made using a loop-through lead to the PC printer socket, USB socket, or through a wireless link using radio waves or infrared technology.

Flatbed scanner from Acer

If you intend to print a scanned image on a 300 dpi printer, you don't need to scan at a resolution higher than 300 dpi. If you plan to display your image on the web or on a display monitor, you only need scan your image using a resolution of 72 dpi – anything larger will not improve image quality, just increase the file size.

HP scanner

Installing a scanner

When you add a scanner in Microsoft Windows, usually Windows recognizes that you're adding a scanner and may offer to install the driver for you. Alternatively, you may be asked to insert the disk containing the correct software driver. Consider the installation guidelines on the facing page.

1 Connect your scanner to your PC as directed in the instructions, using either a physical cable that links either to the printer socket or to a USB socket on the PC, or you may opt for a scanner that uses a wireless technology such as radio waves or infrared.

2 Your PC needs to have installed a software program known as the scanner driver. Usually, in Microsoft Windows, when you connect any new device, Windows attempts to recognize the kind of device you're installing and tries to install the correct driver. Sometimes, however, Windows may ask you to insert a disk containing the latest driver provided by the scanner maker.

Before connecting and installing a new scanner, first make sure you have removed all packaging. Also unlock the transport lock, that holds the scan head safely in position during transit. For normal scanning, the transport lock should be open/released. Check you documentation.

3 Install the scanner as directed in the maker's instructions.

4 After the scanner driver is installed, you'll probably need to restart your PC to ensure Microsoft Windows is updated to include the new scanner.

If when you try to scan a document Microsoft Windows displays a 'Cannot find scanner...' error message, try making sure you switch on the scanner before the PC. Most scanners need to be powered up before the PC, so that Windows can correctly validate the scanner.

5 To confirm that your scanner is installed properly and functioning correctly, perform a test scan. Usually, you'll need to make sure your scanner is switched on before your PC (see margin). A successful test scan ensures that the scanner and PC can communicate correctly.

If you have an earlier version of Windows than Windows 95 or when installing an older scanner, you may need to install the scanner driver manually. Check your Microsoft Windows and scanner documentation to learn what steps you need to take to correctly install and test your scanner.

Installing a digital camera

A digital camera enables you to take photos and use them in documents you create on your computer. You won't need to use camera film, or pay for developing. A recent report suggests that by 2005, more digital cameras will be sold than conventional cameras.

Most digital cameras also come with a colour Liquid Crystal Display (LCD) viewfinder and built-in or removable card memory to allow a set number of photos to be taken. Also, often, an image editing program may come bundled with your camera, that enables you to easily view and edit the images you capture.

Look at the bestselling book Digital Photography in easy steps.

The higher the resolution, the sharper the captured photos can be. So a camera capable of 1,152 x 864 pixels resolution provides clearer photos than one with 640 x 480. You'll also need to determine the kind of memory the camera has. Most provide a removable storage solution such as SmartMedia cards, Compact Flash cards, or floppy disks.

HP Photosmart 618

Most also now include built-in flash, digital zoom control, and some models even include an additional sound recording option. Stored photos can then be transferred to the computer. Most digital cameras now connect to a PC using the ever popular Universal Serial Bus (USB) connector, the serial port, or may use a wireless technology like infrared or radio waves.

Determine the features you want, then try out several before making your final choice. Follow the installation instructions that come with your camera. Once your camera is properly installed in Windows, test your new camera.

Using handheld computers

Introducing handheld PCs

Handheld PCs come in two main types: PDA and Palm, as examined below. Typically, handhelds are used to provide services to users while on the move, so often contain key software to handle and manage things like email, faxes, appointments, memos, address books, web surfing and so on. Additional desirable software includes: word processing, spreadsheet and database applications.

Also, most handhelds now can be connected to a desktop or notebook PC to share information. Options for entering information into a handheld and making selections include using:

You can combine a PDA with a mobile phone to provide a completely wireless PC. For example: the Psion infrared MC218 PDA allows for a completely wireless connection between the Psion and a mobile phone. The Ericsson MCF218 includes a WAP-compliant browser which can be used to link to a standard (GSM) mobile phone, like one of the Ericsson R range.

- A small keyboard (PDA)

- An electronic pen or stylus (Palm)

- A modem

A variety of operating systems can be used in a handheld computer, including the popular Windows CE – a cut-down version of the Microsoft Windows operating system. Microsoft have also made cut-down versions of their popular Microsoft Office suite available for a range of handhelds.

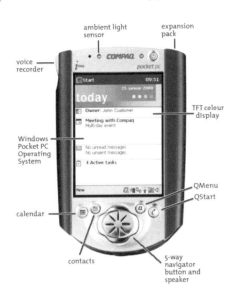

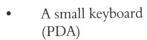

ambient light sensor

expansion pack

voice recorder

TFT colour display

Windows Pocket PC Operating System

QMenu

QStart

calendar

contacts

5-way navigator button and speaker

Introducing the Personal Digital Assistant (PDA)

A Personal Digital Assistant (PDA) is a computing device that is small enough to fit in one hand and which contains a small keyboard to allow data entry. Example PDAs include:

- **Compaq iPAQ:** features include: the Windows Powered Pocket PC operating system and TFT (Thick Film Transistor) colour display. Alternatively, to save money, you can opt for a monochrome model instead.

- **HP Jornada:** Internet-ready colour pocket PC. Includes customised versions of Microsoft Word, Excel, Outlook, Internet Explorer and Media Player.

- **Psion**: keyboard, address book, calendar, word processor, database and spreadsheet.

- **Sony Clié: C**ommunication, **L**ink, **I**nformation and **E**ntertainment (Clié): a handheld computer containing the Palm operating system. Featuring Memory Stick™ technology to store data. Uses 160 x 160 pixels resolution monochrome screen – colour coming soon.

- **Trium Mondo PDA**: combined phone and full-featured PDA.

- **Windows CE:** includes an address book and calendar, word processor, database and spreadsheet; Microsoft PocketPC and Mobile Explorer.

Palm PC basics

Palm computers – often also referred to as palmtops – are a type of handheld computer that includes a stylus or electronic pen in place of a keyboard. Popular palm computers include the Palm III and PalmPilot from 3Com.

Many users buy Palm devices to help with the management of personal information from a portable and easily stored device that has a long battery life, when compared with similar devices. So tools like the address book, calendar, to-do list and memo pad – the content for which can be imported from a desktop PC or Apple Mac – certainly get attention. Out of hours (or not), playing games, listening to MP3 music tracks and reading ebooks also feature high on the popularity list.

Palm devices have found their niche globally – about 13 million are currently in use, or about 80% of the available market: a superb achievement by any standards.

Upgrading your software

Software is a key component that can help make your PC a valuable and productive tool, or provide a series of events that test the limits of your sanity. The software and choice of operating system you choose to install can also make a big difference to efficiency, enjoyment and security of your PC. In this chapter, we'll examine software updates, setting up antivirus and firewall software and how to improve Internet security.

Covers

Chapter Twenty

Performing reliable software updates

Somewhere around the world right now, a software producer is probably either releasing a software update, or is making plans to do so. However, upgrading or installing an operating system or application software may not always go smoothly.

Ideally: develop an effective strategy that can help minimise any possible problems that might occur. Why not take a safe and cautious approach to help prevent delays and minimise any loss or damage to your computer data?

Therefore, consider the following ideas: depending on your particular situation, you may not need to perform all the steps listed. However, do always perform step 1 if you're upgrading an operating system.

Eighteen steps to help ensure trouble-free software upgrading

1. **Backing up:** before installing any software, you may want to back up any files that may be affected by the installation. **This step is even more important if you're upgrading an operating system.** Always ensure the program you use to back up is also compatible with your new operating system – you may need to upgrade or buy alternative backup software before you install a new operating system. You should also test any new or alternative backup software by restoring from older backups on CD-ROMs, disks and tapes.

2. **Be confident:** if you're unsure or uncomfortable about installing software, consider asking a qualified computer technician to install the software for you – always a better option than risking damage to your system.

3. **Antivirus updates:** make sure your antivirus software database – the list of computer viruses against which you're protected – is updated regularly, ideally at least once a week and certainly once every three weeks.

4. **Scan for viruses:** before running any new software setup program, use your antivirus software to scan your new

software, just to make sure that it does not contain any nasty hidden viruses. Also, do the same for any new data files or images that you receive on a regular basis.

5. **Read the instructions:** always read, understand and follow the maker's installation instructions before you start.

6. **Relax:** install new software only when you're not tired and are mentally calm. You may need to concentrate more than you might imagine.

7. **Antivirus/firewall software: off or on?:** if you have antivirus software running 'in the background' automatically, you may need to temporarily disable it before running the new software setup program. You may also likewise need to disable any firewall software temporarily. Check the documentation first though.

8. **Hardware specifications:** ensure your computer system meets ALL the minimum requirements of the new software: CPU, amount of RAM, hard drive space required, and so on. If unsure, check with your software supplier, computer dealer or computer repairer.

9. **Installed older software:** evaluate how any older software that you may already have installed will behave after you install the new software. For example, some older programs may not function with a new operating system.

10. **In business:** for work-related software upgrades, aim to install at the start of your working day, or earlier, to minimise any disruption to business. Also, you're more likely to get quick access to professional help during business hours should you need it. Before starting, make doubly sure the essential backups have been completed and tested.

11. **Using a test system:** if the upgrade is particularly large or crucial to a business system or process, why not perform a series of test installations using different options on a similar PC or small network first to get familiar with the process and highlight any unforeseen problems. This way, your main PC system is not affected by any glitches. Then, when ready, you can install on the main computer system.

12. **Existing software:** for existing, critical business software, contact the software supplier and tell them what you are doing. Determine whether what you want to do will affect any other software and if so, discover what those effects are before installing your new software.

13. **Installation or upgrade:** install the new software according to the maker's instructions.

14. **Rebooting:** after the new software is installed, reboot (restart) your computer. If Microsoft Windows asks you to reboot your PC, it's not a bad idea to reboot twice. Why? To make absolutely sure that the update has been completed properly. After the first reboot, remember Microsoft Windows will only restart properly next time provided the PC is shut down normally. The second reboot ensures the update is registered correctly.

15. **Performing first checks:** ensure that the PC is working correctly. If you're in business, make sure your essential business-related software applications are working correctly. Test them properly: don't just try one or two functions.

16. **New documentation:** read the manuals, Help files and 'quick' guides. Run any demos. Get familiar with the new software.

17. **New backups:** make a backup of your new software as soon as possible. Do not, at this stage, erase your old backups. Instead, start new ones.

18. **User training:** ensure all other users know how to use the new software. Allow a generous amount of training time initially to avoid all kinds of new problems later.

Preparing a PC for the Internet

The Internet offers a huge range of possibilities. However, to benefit most, you'll need to have your PC protected and set up correctly. Consider the following ideas:

1. **Protect your PC from computer viruses:** make sure you use a regularly updated antivirus software package, that also checks email messages too. See page 172 for details.

2. **Install a firewall:** either as software or hardware. For more information, see page 177.

3. **Find a low-cost, fixed-price Internet Service Provider:** more and more ISPs are now providing some great package deals so you won't have any unexpected, large phone bills. For example: BT Internet AnyTime package.

You'll need an Internet-compatible PC. Any Pentium or Pentium-equivalent PC with at least 16Mb of RAM should be fine. However, with today's interactive web pages, the faster your CPU, and the more RAM installed, the more stable will be your web viewing experience.

3. **Choose a default web browser:** Microsoft Windows 95/98/Me/XP/2000 comes with Internet Explorer web browser built in. Or why not try out Netscape Communicator or Opera 5 from Opera Software?

4. **Install an email program:** Outlook Express comes with Windows 95/98/Me/XP/2000. Other popular options are available from Netscape, Eudora and Pegasus.

5. **Install a news reader:** in order to access over 65,000 newsgroups on the Internet. Microsoft News comes as part of the Outlook Express email program that is part of the Windows operating system. Other options include Agent from www.forteinc.com/. For access and setup details, check with your Internet Service Provider.

6. **Install an FTP program:** to enable you to download and upload files and software to and from the Internet.

AGENT NEWS & MAIL READER

▣ AGENT - THE #1 NEWS AND MAIL READER ON THE INTERNET

Do you need a good way to read Internet newsgroups without having to sift through all the fluff? If you spend a lot of time trying to find the information that interests you, be sure to check out Agent, the most popular online/offline news and mail reader software on the Internet. Agent and its freeware version, Free Agent, are available for Windows in 16-bit and 32-bit versions. These products make it easy and efficient to collect and organize your news and they can save you money by allowing you to read mail and news offline!

Design and Development

Dreamweaver 4
Make short work of Web site and HTML page production.

Fireworks 4
Design and optimize Web graphics for easy integration into your site.

Dreamweaver UltraDev 4
Develop database-driven Web applications in a visual environment (using ASP, JSP and CFML).

HomeSite
Code HTML quickly with this lightweight text editor.

CAUTION: choose your sources well: some files can contain hidden computer viruses.

7. **Website software:** why not create and upload your own website. You can learn all about web design in *Web Page Design in easy steps* (www.ineasysteps.com/).

8. **Stay in touch – instantly:** to really join the 'cutting edge', why not install a web cam and instant messaging software like Microsoft Netmeeting?

Web cam from

Logitech

Combating PC theft

PCs, Pentium-type CPUs and RAM all command high resale values and so attract thieves without much hesitation. However, often, the most valuable part of a PC is the data which it contains. Therefore, perform regular backups using methods like those discussed in Chapter Seven.

Nevertheless, there is much you can do to deter thieves. We can never prevent theft but we can, as with all good antitheft devices and procedures, make the task so difficult that our imaginary thief would rather choose an easier option.

Consider installing special software that renders a PC's hard drive useless unless a special code is entered – and advertise this fact prominently on the PC's outer cover.

Many devices are available, from high-tech PC alarms to a simple but often effective 'bolt it to the desk' approach. Also, don't forget the simple deterrent of keeping a PC covered when not in use: if a thief doesn't know a PC is present, he may not bother to find out.

One solution from SecurityWare: Universal kit 2

You can ensure your data is kept safe and private by using an encryption password program. The author uses a program called Windows Enforcer, available from Posum software at: www.posum.com

PC security is easy to ignore or overlook. For a few pounds though you could provide a high level of protection and help deter thieves from targeting your PC. The following paragraphs list some current approaches to combating computer theft.

Protecting your RAM memory – one approach
One popular approach used by RAM IC manufacturers and subsidiaries involves electronically tagging RAM chips and attaching an identifying label. If a thief then attempts to remove the label the RAM chip is immediately rendered useless, which for the thief is rather discouraging.

Protecting your PC, monitor and printer
A common method of protecting an entire PC is to install an alarm in the form of a plug-in expansion card – like *PC Protector*. When activated, these alarms usually provide a deafening 100+ decibels sound level – about as loud as a small fire alarm – and usually sound for about one minute – long enough to deter most thieves.

Power from these card-based alarms usually comes from their own rechargeable battery. An ideal PC alarm system should include as many of the following features as possible:

- Alarm sounds if PC is dismantled

- Alarm sounds if RAM is removed

- Alarm sounds if the CPU chip is removed

Whatever measures you take to protect your PC, the only way to safeguard your data is to regularly perform effective up-to-date backups. For any business, this is essential.

- Alarm sounds if the cables are disconnected

- Alarm sounds if the PC is moved

- Protection for the monitor and printer through an interconnecting cable

If you carry computer equipment in cars, cover the equipment when away from your car or, better still, take it with you ideally in a plain-type travel bag! Notebook PC bags immediately alert potential thieves as to what you're carrying.

- Provision of an override in the form of a special security key, in case the alarm is accidentally triggered

Finding a stolen PC containing an internal modem

For PCs with an internal modem, Kestrel Software Systems have come up with an ingenious and interesting approach to help track down a PC if it gets stolen. Their approach assumes the thieves will at some stage connect the PC modem to the phone line.

Once installed, the software is 'invisible'. Each time the PC is switched on, the 'invisible' software dials a specified number at a specified time every day: this could be your own home or office number.

In normal operation, each time the modem dials your own number, it will of course receive an engaged tone and so will disconnect. However, if the PC is stolen, the modem only has to make one successful call, after which you can dial 1471 (in the UK) to find the number to which the modem is currently connected, and quickly inform the police. The program is called ETPH (ET Phones Home) and may be available as shareware from Kestrel Software Systems Ltd.

How to prevent mobile computer theft

If you use a mobile PC, you're a prime target. Often, thieves like to work in small groups – one to distract you, one to steal the PC and one to pass it on to quickly. The list below covers most areas that most of us become involved in today, so just what steps can we take to minimise portable PC theft? Consider the ideas below and those in the margin. Especially lucrative locations for thieves include:

Portable computers should include several levels of password protection or a security lock. Possible levels should ideally include: administrator, (BIOS) set-up, Power-on and hard drive access. See Beware Tip below.

On a portable PC with password protection, usually, the administrator and hard drive passwords are the most powerful, effective and potentially the most devastating. WARNING: if you forget or lose these kinds of passwords, you may have two or three tries before the system shuts down and you may not be able to access your hard drive ever, even if it is moved to another PC! The idea is to protect access to your data.

- **Airports:** favourite scam: happens at the X-ray scanner. Both will try to stand immediately in front of you in the queue. The first one goes through normally while the second uses a delay excuse (lost keys, search in pockets, etc.). Now you're delayed while the first thief grabs your notebook that has just gone through the scanner. Be aware: as far as is possible, do not let go of your PC until you're sure you're in a safe location.

- **Train stations:** always keep hold of your PC while waiting for your train.

- **Car parks:** don't ever leave a PC in a vehicle.

- **Hotels:** don't leave a PC in a hotel room. Lock your room at night. Caution: open ground-floor windows.

- **Offices:** use authorized entry systems. Log all who enter and leave. Use video surveillance systems.

- **Homes:** use a burglar alarm and prominently display an alarm bell or box outside. Lock windows and doors when leaving – even for a short time.

- **Traffic hold-ups:** don't leave a PC or notebook case openly displayed. Also, lock your car doors from inside to reduce possible hit-and-run snatch attacks.

- **Any public buildings or thoroughfares:** especially busy areas make ideal thieving ground.

- **While walking along any public street:** consider using a plain padded bag or lockable briefcase rather than a PC bag that identifies you have a portable computer.

Using antivirus software

What is a computer virus?

Any software program that upsets or interferes with the normal operation of your PC can be defined as a virus. Many different types of virus exist, but essentially they can have two main effects:

- Display annoying, often misleading messages on your screen, but which leave your data/applications intact.

- Damage your PC's data and/or software applications permanently or share your data with unauthorised users (usually via the Internet).

How to catch a virus

The Boot Sector or Boot Record is the first sector on a hard drive or partition that contains the key information to enable a PC to function.

The only way to catch a virus is to copy and run an infected program. A virus-infected program can be copied using floppy diskettes, direct PC-to-PC connection, using the Internet or accepting email (see below). A virus can be hidden in the boot sector of a hard drive, embedded in the code of a program, or disguised in macros such as those used in Microsoft Word and Excel.

However, it's important to note that, to date, a virus can't usually be passed on in a pure unopened email message. But a virus could be hidden in a binary (program) file attached to an email: for example, someone sending a Microsoft Word document containing an infected macro. The Internet is now also a major source of concern, as a virus could be hidden in Java applets, ActiveX modules or even HTML newsletters.

Finding antivirus software

You can visit your local computer supplier, check reviews in PC magazines and download antivirus software from the web, including:

- Norton Antivirus: www.symantec.com/

- McAfee: www.mcafee.com/

- InnoculateIT: antivirus.cai.com/

- Sophos Antivirus: www.sophos.com/

Do use a regularly updated antivirus program to provide the best protection for your PC and precious data. The key word here is 'regularly'.

You download when you take something off the Internet and store it on your PC. When you transfer something to the Internet, you're uploading.

Download antivirus updates ideally every two weeks at least. Most antivirus software can be set up to remind you at specified intervals.

So why do we feel it so important to run up-to-date antivirus software? More and more people today are sharing computer files. One statistic suggests that email and Internet downloads are responsible for 75% of all viruses.

A virus could be hidden in small Internet-related files called cookies, that are often automatically copied to your hard drive when you visit many websites. However, most website owners keen to build their web businesses take particular care to prevent this from happening.

This scenario may become even worse as the Internet continues to integrate with the daily life of more and more people. So we need to be on our guard not only to resist virus infection but also to combat the ever growing number of sometimes equally damaging computer virus hoaxes.

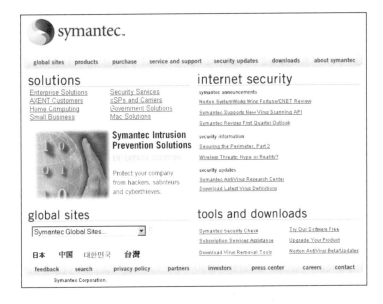

An antivirus approach

One of the simplest remedies is to back up your data; then back up and back up again. Get in the habit of backing up your data regularly. But if you become aware of contracting a computer virus, don't do any more backups until the virus has been *completely* removed from your PC or network. Keep your backups safe until you're sure the virus has been *totally* removed!

If possible, store your data in a separate location to your applications.
Why: to help make the task of recovering your information easier if your PC picks up a virus. Example: if your PC has two partitions named drive C: and drive D:, perhaps keep all your data on drive D: and all applications on drive C:.

If you receive any unsolicited disks through the post with which you're not familiar, simply don't use them.

Obtain and use a dedicated and regularly updated antivirus software package. That is, one which thoroughly checks *everything* that is saved to your hard drive, especially any files downloaded from the Internet.

Provided you choose one of the proven antivirus software
packages, which one you choose is perhaps not as important as performing regular updates to its antivirus tables (the database in your antivirus program that displays the number and type of viruses against which you're protected).

Good antivirus software providers often make available updates on their websites covering the latest viruses. In this way, you can buy an antivirus package and still be assured you're covered by downloading the updates when necessary. *This is an excellent way to ensure you get as much protection as you possibly can*.

McAfee and Symantec are two well-known antivirus software providers who both provide updates on their websites. Dr. Solomon's antivirus package is also very popular.

Key point: any antivirus software is perhaps only as effective as the updates downloaded within the last 1–4 weeks. Why? Most of the virus threats come from newer viruses, not older ones for which the remedies are probably already installed in antivirus packages.

Dealing with a computer virus

For most people, viruses are more hype than reality, but don't try and tell that to the small business owner whose business was decimated by a computer virus.

Is it a virus? Checking for virus hoaxes

Virus hoaxes can cause as much disruption. For those bent on causing havoc, sometimes, the fear of a computer virus is just as effective as the virus itself. So these folks try to use the age-old tools of ignorance and fear to tell us that we're infected with the 'XYZ' virus, when we're simply not. Fortunately, several generous reputable website providers include lists of all the latest virus hoaxes. For example:

*   **Virus myths:** check out www.vmyths.com

*   **Virus hoaxes:** check out HoaxBusters at HoaxBusters.ciac.org

*   **The UK Financial Services Authority:** www.fsa.gov.uk/

*   **The Fraud Information Centre:** www.fraud.org/

*   **Scambusters:** www.scambusters.com/

Alternatively, simply check with your favourite antivirus supplier who may also provide information on the latest hoaxes.

If the worst happens...

If you're unfortunate enough to experience a computer virus infection, it's difficult to provide one single method of recovery, as each situation will probably be different. However, as a general guide, consider the following ideas:

1   Don't panic: easy to say, I know, but it really is crucial that you try to remain as calm as possible to avoid an (understandable) knee-jerk reaction.

2   At this stage, don't make any changes to your system, unless you really know what you're doing and why you're doing it.

3   If you have up-to-date antivirus software installed, your software
    may have detected the virus, identified it by name, and may offer
    options including quarantine or deletion. Usually best to follow the
    advice provided.

4   If your antivirus program cannot suggest a remedy, check its user
    guide and, if possible, the program's Help file to determine what
    action to take next.

5   Check out the newsgroups: ask a friend or colleague with a virus-
    free PC to access the newsgroup: alt.comp.virus Other users who
    may also have been infected may suggest quick remedies.

6   If you can still access the Internet, some antivirus software makers
    provide virus detection services that can check your system live
    online and help remove a virus. For example, check out
    www.housecall.antivirus.com/ or the McAfee Online Clinic at
    www.mcafee.com/

7   If the problem remains and your data is particularly valuable, you
    could benefit by discussing options with a reputable professional
    expert. If your backups are almost up to date, first make further
    backup copies of your backups. Your expert then might suggest (1)
    completely reformatting your PC's hard drive, (2) making absolutely
    sure the virus is destroyed, (3) re-installing the operating system, (4)
    re-installing your backup software, and (5) restoring your system
    from your most recent backups. A time-consuming procedure, but
    one that in extreme circumstances may sometimes offer the only
    real practical option remaining.

Protecting your PCs with a firewall

The subject of firewalls is a complex and in-depth topic so in these pages we can only outline basic ideas that might be worth investigating for users of single PC or those with small networks of up to four PCs.

For maximum security and up-to-date information about what's currently on offer, discuss your precise needs with a reputable firewall consultant.

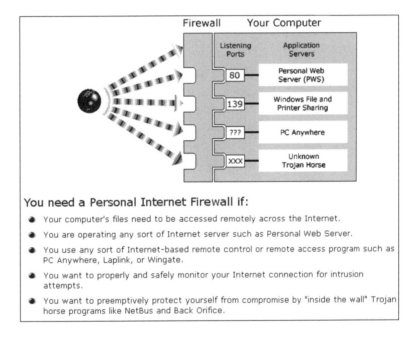

You need a Personal Internet Firewall if:

- Your computer's files need to be accessed remotely across the Internet.
- You are operating any sort of Internet server such as Personal Web Server.
- You use any sort of Internet-based remote control or remote access program such as PC Anywhere, Laplink, or Wingate.
- You want to properly and safely monitor your Internet connection for intrusion attempts.
- You want to preemptively protect yourself from compromise by "inside the wall" Trojan horse programs like NetBus and Back Orifice.

GRC.com: a superb free information resource

What is a firewall?

In a PC context, a firewall is a barrier to prevent someone accessing the files on your PC without your knowledge or permission. Two kinds of firewall are available today:

- **Software-based:** several firewall software products are now available but some may be better than others. For example, the popular Norton Internet Security software provides a 2-in-1 antivirus and firewall solution. Or, if you're looking for a firewall solution only, why not also check out ZoneAlarm (www.zonelabs.com/) BlackICE Defender (www.networkice.com/) or McAfee Firewall (www.mcafee.com/). Note: usually, the most recent versions provide the best protection.

- **Hardware-based:** nothing to configure, no extra software to slow down a computer, and simple to use. This option is especially useful for those who spend many hours permanently connected to the Internet. Examples include: cable modem, ISDN or ADSL users.

Using a router to protect a small network

One option that might be suitable for a small network is to use a router to provide a hardware-based firewall. This allows several computers to share the same Internet connection, while providing firewall protection to all computers on the network without having to install any extra software.

Firewall software is available from a range of makers.

Reviews in PC magazines provide one of the best ways to help evaluate what is most suitable for your particular situation.

How to avoid being scanned on the Internet

While online and using the Internet, perhaps especially if you're using a typical (unprotected) Microsoft Windows installation, there's a good chance that your computer is being scanned or probed by someone somewhere without your permission.

People who probably don't have your best interests at heart are running Internet scanners 24 hours continuously. Their aim: to use their scanning software to 'sniff' out interesting information. For example, they're particularly interested in folder names or key words like: 'accounts', 'passwords', 'private', and so on. They get this information by coming into your PC while you're online, perhaps using any one of your computer's 64,000 ports (access gateways).

A correctly set up firewall however can prevent anyone entering your PC without your permission. After installing the wonderful ZoneAlarm (www.zonelabs.com/), the author was amazed at the quantity of attempted intrusions. To date, ZoneAlarm Pro v2.6.84 has been 100% successful!

Evaluating firewall software and testing your PC

Several basic firewall software programs are available for download from the Internet. Steve Gibson at the Gibson Research Corporation at grc.com/ provides what is probably one of the best plain English website resources available for anyone seeking to know more about firewalls and to compare features, benefits and drawbacks of the popular current offerings. Also check out grc.com/lt/scoreboard.htm

The website is also ideal if you want to check out how secure your PC is while connected to the Internet. Many

Internet Connection Security for Windows Users
by Steve Gibson, Gibson Research Corporation

readers, I suspect, will be shocked by the results – especially if an effective firewall is not already in place. Therefore, why not simply go to grc.com, check out the 'Shields Up' option and let the website test your computer for free. Then certainly take note of the superb free information and guidelines generously provided.

Aiming for maximum protection

Today, the Internet offers an amazingly interesting 'landscape'. However, if you go in unprotected, you're leaving open potentially thousands of doors (ports), any one of which might allow a scanner to enter your PC.

For best results, combine a firewall with proven antivirus software that you update regularly – ideally every one or two weeks.

For the last few years, the author has successfully used ZoneAlarm Pro firewall software in combination with the well designed Norton Antivirus – updated each week – to provide a 99%+ successful solution against intrusion – the one that did get through occurred when my antivirus software was mistakenly turned off. Remedy: benefit from my mistake: ensure your antivirus software is *always* active while your PC is switched on.

Using Internet content control software

Although interesting and amazing, the Internet is a wild 'land' containing many sources of information, pictures and videos that are meant for opt-in adult viewing only. Key point: parents should monitor their children while they browse the web to avoid any nasty surprises.

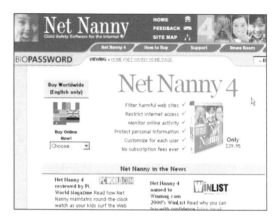

Responsible web browser makers like Microsoft (Internet Explorer) and Netscape (Navigator) do provide commands that can allow restrictions to be placed on the kind of information users may access on the web. These controls typically allow you to monitor and set levels for bad language, nudity, sex and violence.

You can also buy powerful third-party standalone software like Cyber Patrol (www.cyberpatrol.com) and Net Nanny (www.netnanny.com) to help further manage and filter web content viewing to ensure you only see the kind of websites you want to see.

Nevertheless, do not rely totally on any content control software to manage your child's web viewing. No software is perfect and may not function in the way we might expect in every instance. Ideally, get involved with your child to periodically evaluate what they are viewing.

Fine-tuning your PC

Once you've upgraded your PC, often there are still further ways in which you can enhance and protect your investment or improve the way your PC works. In this final chapter, we examine several ways in which you can get the best out of your PC.

Covers

Chapter Twenty-one

Maximising the useful life of your PC

Dealing with dust

Over time, dust builds up in a PC and tends to act as an insulator, often reducing components' ability to dissipate heat. This interferes with cooling and can cause several problems. If too much heat builds up, the useful life-span of electronic components is reduced as they can then overheat.

Before clearing away the dust build-up from a PC, make sure the PC is switched off and that your antistatic wrist strap is fitted before you remove the case cover (see page 14 for more information about taking antistatic precautions).

Cigarette smoke can be particularly damaging to PCs. The smoke may contain elements that can accelerate corrosion and produce additional conductive pathways on circuit boards where there should be none.

Use canned compressed air to clear away the build-up of dust from inside the PC, particularly near the expansion slots, CPU and power-supply fan vents. Don't spray anywhere near your eyes. Ideally, buy only compressed air that is designed for cleaning a computer system. Sometimes, a burst of compressed air can also produce an accompanying electrical static charge which could damage components. Makers of this special canned compressed air are aware of this problem and design their product to compensate for it.

Floppy disk, CD-/DVD-ROM and internal tape drives

Floppy drives and tape drives provide two of the main access points for dust and debris to enter a PC. CD-/DVD-ROM drives, to a certain extent, also represent an easy entry path for dust. Again, use the special canned compressed air to clear the area, especially around the tray-loading section; but be careful not to spray near laser lenses: these electronic assemblies are very sensitive and can easily be damaged.

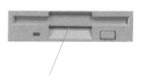

Gently lift the floppy drive flap and spray compressed air here in short bursts.

Open the CD-ROM drive tray, remove the CD-ROM and spray around the loading tray area. Take care to avoid spraying the laser lens assembly.

Hard drives

Hard drives are designed as sealed units and should never be opened unless carrying out a service or data-recovery operation. All hard drives should include a special filter which ensures that dust can't enter the inner drive assembly. Therefore, from a cleaning aspect, simply blow any dust present away from the drive connectors using the canned compressed air available from computer stores.

Switch it off or leave it on?

Many people are concerned about whether to leave a PC switched on when it's not being used. This is not an easy question to answer. Most modern PCs often include energy-saving features which can usually ensure a PC 'sleeps' after a period of non-use. However, this option still doesn't really answer the question of whether to switch it off when not in use. Let's deal with that next.

Electronic components are at their most stressed when a device is switching on or off. Once a PC has been running for a few minutes, the variation of heat given off by components starts to stabilise. Therefore, arguably, to maximise component life, the best solution would be to leave the PC on as long as possible. Often and for safety reasons, this option may not be a practical one.

As an author, I am constantly using my PC. I built my entire PC to my own specification using the knowledge provided in this book. However, there are times, perhaps for 2–3 hours during the day, when my PC isn't being used.

High on my list of priorities was an energy-saving feature. As my PC and monitor are Energy Star-compliant, I can set up the BIOS and Windows to detect when the PC is not being used. If it is left idle for six minutes, the PC enters sleep mode.

The energy consumption in sleep mode is very small, and this also lengthens the useful life of the PC.

SAVING THE EARTH. SAVING YOUR MONEY.

I switch the PC on at the start of my working day, and switch it off at the end: in this way, energy consumption is minimised when the PC is not in use, yet the stresses put upon electronic components are reduced and the system is always in a 'pre-charged' state when not being used during the working day. As a result, reliability has been and remains high.

If your system is not Energy Star compliant, one of the best ways of saving energy while keeping stresses to a minimum is to simply switch only the monitor off when the PC is not used during the working day. However, do remember that there are safety aspects to consider when leaving a PC switched on unattended. If you're not happy about this, it's always better to switch everything off.

As all electronic components create heat, and it is heat which essentially erodes the useful life of your components, the aim is to reduce the amount of heat and radiation produced. PC makers are constantly striving to find new ways in which to save power. The best ones carry the important logos shown on previous pages and also those below.

Reorganising a hard drive

File fragmentation

It's amazing how quickly you can fill up the space on a hard drive. To make matters worse, Microsoft Windows usually stores information wherever there's space available. This means that often files can become fragmented: different parts of the same file may be stored in different locations on a hard drive. This means that the next time you want to view the file, your PC has to search different locations to find all the components that make up that particular file; it simply takes longer to find the information.

Always back up your PC before manipulating or changing the way data is stored on your hard drive and especially if you plan to repartition a hard drive.

Windows 98/Me/XP includes some great tools that can automatically prevent the build up of fragmented files. Windows 95 (and earlier versions) requires a strategy.

Why bother to repartition a hard drive?

Many PCs tend to have a single hard drive partition; this can be quite wasteful for the reason mentioned above. If your PC uses the 16-bit FAT (File Allocation Table) system, found in operating systems such as DOS, Windows 3.x and some versions of Windows 95, and your hard drive is over 1Gb, then a surprising amount of space could be being wasted, simply due to the size of the partition(s).

If you upgrade to Windows 98/Me/XP and opt to use the FAT32 system, file defragmentation problems are much reduced if you use the tools provided within the operating system. With Windows 2000, the native NTFS is an even better option to help minimise file fragmentation.

If you're using an operating system based on this earlier FAT16 system, by repartitioning a hard drive you may be able to reclaim hundreds of megabytes of wasted space.

Normally, when you repartition, all the data is automatically lost. However, utilities are now available that enable you to repartition 'on the fly'. Of course, to do this, you have to be sure the program does what it claims to do, as the risks are great if things go wrong and you've not backed up your PC (see Beware Tip in margin).

How a FAT16-based PC can waste space

A cluster is the smallest unit of data a PC can use. If a file or part of a file takes up less space than a cluster, it still requires a cluster. Usually, 16-bit FAT hard drives of between 1Gb and 2Gb use 32Kb clusters. So for a file of only 3Kb in size, it still takes up 32Kb.

Imagine how much space is wasted if the majority of your files are quite small. Hard drive sizes between 512Kb and 1Gb usually use

16Kb cluster sizes, which is better: using the scenario above, this time the wasted space is a maximum 16Kb instead of 32Kb.

The table below illustrates the exact relationship between cluster size and hard drive size up to about 2Gb in size when using the older 16-bit FAT system.

If you decide to repartition, take some time to reconsider the structure of your directories and files. PartitionMagic also includes Uninstaller Mover, which can make the process of moving entire directories and files between partitions much easier.

How cluster size relates to hard drive size	
Size of hard drive	Cluster size
16Mb-127Mb	2Kb
128Mb-255Mb	4Kb
256Mb-511Mb	8Kb
512Mb-1,023Mb	16Kb
1,024Mb-2,047Mb	32Kb

Thankfully, the FAT32 system used in Windows 98/Me/XP and optionally in Windows 2000 can use smaller clusters – typically 4Kb – creating less wasted space.

Hard drive partitions larger than 2Gb aren't supported in FAT16, and those smaller than 512Mb are not supported in FAT32.

Off-the-shelf partitioning utilities

PartitionMagic from PowerQuest and other similar tried and tested utilities allow you to carry out all sorts of tasks easily which would otherwise be very time-consuming and lengthy.

PartitionMagic allows you to reclaim disk space wasted through having large partitions in FAT16, organise and protect your data, and run multiple operating systems safely on the same PC. *Partition-it* from Quarterdeck and *Partition Commander* are two other popular on-the-fly partitioning utilities.

Index

T

U

V

W